KISS
THE MAGNOLIA
TREE

R. Douglas White

ISBN 978-1-63814-238-6 (Paperback)
ISBN 978-1-63814-239-3 (Digital)

All quotes are from the New King James Bible,
Thomas Nelson Publishers, Nashville, Tennessee.

Covenant Books
11661 Hwy 707
Murrells Inlet, SC 29576
www.covenantbooks.com

To all the constructive women, north and south,
who work to build up their communities

KISS
THE MAGNOLIA
TREE

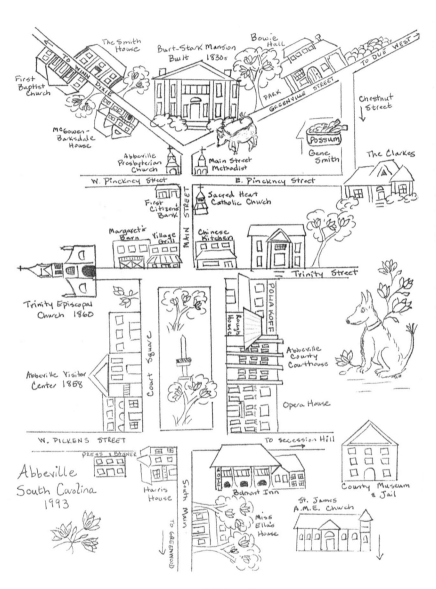

Map of Abbeville

1

Abbeville, South Carolina
September 1993

The afternoon was hot and dry. The crape myrtle blossoms blew across the old carriage driveway. A large magnolia tree shaded the porch from the westward setting sun. The first week of graduate school was over, and I had survived. Taking the year off from my counseling practice was much needed, even though my family thought I had lost my mind. It had been three years since my wife Laura had died.

I rocked as I daydreamed. I sat on one side of the large porch as the last tour group had gone into the Burt-Stark Mansion. Several years before, I had taken the same tour and heard about the night Jefferson Davis and his war cabinet met there and decided to discontinue the War for Southern Independence. I rocked back and forth, thinking only of the dusty mist. My thoughts were briefly interrupted by the buzzing of several bees. Beyond the boxwoods and crape myrtles lining the driveway, I could see the numerous church spires along the street coming up to the mansion. A sweet smell filled the air. I enjoyed the ease of an afternoon with no calls, no clients, and no classes.

Through my daydreaming and the calm of the hot afternoon, I could hear the voice of a woman asking me if she could share the porch. Before I could respond, she sat down and began to rock. As the rate of her rocking increased, I was jarred out of my daydreaming. She introduced herself as a married cousin of Miss Ella Perrin Cox.

She announced that she was a Northerner. As I tried to gather my thoughts, I asked her if that was a problem. She replied that it would be if the Abbeville ladies knew her secret. I started to rock again. We talked of the heat, the very dry summer, and the deer coming into town and eating everyone's flowers.

The woman told me she was waiting for Miss Ella and then informed me that Ella was a direct descendant of Mr. Thomas Chiles Perrin, a signer of the Ordinance of Secession. The woman was dressed in dull gray cotton pants that did not match the dresses of ladies I had met in Abbeville. As we both rocked, she asked me if I could keep a secret. She seemed to want to confess something, so I agreed to keep her secret. There was silence. Then she related that if I told her secret, the "ladies" of Abbeville would never speak to her again. I kept silent and waited for her confession. She spoke more quietly and stated that her ancestor had been a soldier in Sherman's army during the 1865 march through Georgia. I did not know what to say, so she repeated that her ancestor was a Yankee who served under General Sherman, who burned a path across Georgia from Atlanta to Savannah.

When I asked her if Sherman had burned down Abbeville, she stated that he never came to Abbeville but destroyed the South Carolina capital, Columbia. I told her I had been a professional therapist, so confidentiality was my business. I could not resist asking her if she was sure the ladies would not speak to her, since she was a relative of Miss Ella. I reminded her the Perrin family commanded a great deal of respect in town. She replied by asking me how long I had been in Abbeville. When I told her "about one week," she looked straight at me and pulled herself up on the front of the rocking chair. I waited for her to speak. After a time, she declared that if I stayed in Abbeville, I was going to see the ghosts and shadows of old South Carolina. She paused and, looking straight at me, stated, "Abbeville is more Southern than the magnolia tree."

I did not have time to ask questions because the large door of the mansion opened, and out walked the people on the last tour. They were led by a dark collie-looking dog that ran down the front steps and disappeared.

Burt-Stark Mansion

2

Soon Miss Ella came out and introduced herself. I stood up as I had been taught to do. She was a small lady with perfectly curled white-blonde hair. She spoke with a thick South Carolina accent and smiled as she talked. She seemed anxious, but I learned later she always seemed excited when she spoke. She asked if I was waiting for Margaret to finish. I replied that I was just enjoying the afternoon and that I had met her relative. Miss Ella invited me to go eat with them, but I told her I was going to a play at the Abbeville Opera House. They excused themselves and walked down the stairs. Miss Ella's cousin turned back to me at one point and put her finger to her lips.

As I was about to sit down, Miss Margaret came out of the mansion. She was smiling at first and asked if I had met Ella and her relative. I said I had. Miss Margaret stated that she was going to the lake to meet some friends for the weekend and asked if I would feed her two dogs, because the gardener did not work on weekends. The conversation was formal until she started talking about the Burt-Stark Mansion. She was glad I was visiting the house. She said she grew up while Mary Stark lived there. She even remembered Mr. and Mrs. Stark Sr., Mary's parents. She explained that Mrs. Stark Sr. was a niece of Mrs. Burt, who had entertained President Jefferson Davis.

It was Mrs. Stark Sr. who restored the house as she remembered from 1865. People gossiped that Mary would sunbathe in the nude, but this was just "trashy talk." In a softer voice, Miss Margaret said the beautiful Stark sisters were "private and proper ladies." She stated that gossip was an epidemic problem in Abbeville. She went on to say that the sisters, Mary and Fanny, left the house, furniture, and carriage driveway park to show how Southern aristocrats lived and in memory of Mr. Davis. She added that Mrs. Varina Davis, the president's wife, spent two weeks at the mansion before Mr. Davis arrived. She stated: "This is a very important place."

Margaret stopped a moment but then started talking about the party she was giving at her lake house. She told me to say hello to Jack and Evelyn Cauley when I saw them at the play. I asked her if I could drive her to her house, but she said she liked the walk. When I got to my car, I observed Miss Margaret walking up Greenville Street. She was a woman in her early eighties, but her posture was that of a youth. Following behind her was the brown-and-black dog I saw coming out of the mansion earlier. They resembled a small victory parade. The dog pranced behind her with its long nose high in the air and its tail wagging. Miss Margaret called the dog Possum. With the long nose and brush-like tail, the dog looked like a possum indeed.

3

This encounter with Mrs. Margaret Bowie—a longtime widow, referred to by all as Miss Margaret—was in sharp contrast to my first meeting earlier in the summer. My first impression of Miss Margaret came from a formal interview I had with her about renting a room in her house. The Clarkes, who had recommended me to her, told me Miss Margaret was fearful of living alone.

She sat on a Victorian chair by the fireplace; I sat on an antique Empire sofa. She explained that she grew up on Magazine Street in Abbeville, but she had lived in this house since the late 1930s. She then went into a history of the 1944 storm that killed so many people in South Carolina. She stated that she did not like living in this large house alone. I could tell that she had fears.

Miss Margaret had the manicured look of a Southern lady. Though her features were small, her chin was strong. She had bright eyes with a perfectly proportioned nose for her small face. Her hair was not rigidly set but gently curved around her face. Her silky gray hair was highlighted by small strands of white. She stood about five foot four. Her voice had a certain allure. It was smooth, precise, and Southern. Every word carried a warm, elongated tone. As she talked about the rules of her house, Bowie Hall, I became aware that her calmness covered a determination to have things done in a proper manner. I knew not to mistake her seeming warmth for weakness. Later, I would hear her say, "If I do not set a standard in Abbeville, who will?"

That day, I agreed to the terms of the rental agreement. At the end of the interview, she said I could bring my dog. Her offer made me happy, since Sugar Baby and I were a team. By this understanding, Sugar Baby and I came to be residents of Bowie Hall on Greenville Street. Our residence was almost next door to the historic Burt-Stark Mansion.

At the time of my wife's death three years before, I promised her I would take care of our dog, Sugar Baby. Bringing my dog to Bowie Hall was a solution. My plans to return to graduate school had come together. I really needed to take one year off from my counseling practice.

4

As I finished recollecting my rental interview with Miss Margaret, I realized how hot it was in my Jeep and turned on the air conditioner. As I sat there waiting for the car to cool, I thought how different the past week had been. For twenty-three years I worked with people and their emotional problems, I had never heard the phrase "private and proper" used to describe a person. Miss Ella's cousin had warned me that I would see shadows of the past.

As I drove out of Greenville Street and then turned onto North Main, I looked back at the mansion. One lone magnolia tree was anchored in front of the house. I thought that it seemed out of place, since some of its branches were gone. It must have been a very old tree. Traveling up North Main Street, I noticed many different fine houses and large beautiful trees. The hot wind moved the trees back and forth. I thought a storm was brewing, but there was only wind. I slowed down as I passed a woman with a baby stroller. She waved, and I returned the gesture.

As I rode along, there was a large French-style house on the right, and a Gothic-style house stood in a thick grove of trees in the next block. Many large houses had columns. I saw numerous small raised Southern-style cottages. Several brick ranch-style houses appeared. I had learned that the old Rosenberg cottage had been moved to town from the country and now served as an antique shop. It must have had an interesting history. The cottage had the classic four-columned front porch. I passed one of the old Perrin houses and then the Winn-Dixie. The gas station was located several turns away on the bypass. After having a welcoming man pump gas for my car, I returned to Greenville Street. The wind continued to be warm.

That night, I met my friends Jack and Evelyn at the old opera house. Jack Cauley and I had been friends since graduate school in Louisville, Kentucky. Evelyn was his young, beautiful wife who had grown up in the Greenwood area. They were such a fun couple! I also met a number of friends of Miss Margaret. Two of them looked me over and asked if I was able to say no. When I asked why, Miss Sallie McMillan stated that Margaret was a lady who liked directing people. We laughed and moved on.

The Abbeville Opera House stood next to the Belmont Inn. It was constructed in the classical style, while the Belmont was a brick building with a large porch across the front. On the other side of the opera house was the city hall, facing the square. From a wide plaza, one went into the opera house to the ticket area. From there, a set of steps went down to the auditorium. The theatre was built with classic round seating with balconies on each side of the center section. It looked as if it had been built in the nineteenth century, but the stage was quite modern. The building was ornate and beautiful. The present opera house opened in 1908. Abbeville was an overnight stop for traveling theatre troupes that followed the tour circuit from New York to Atlanta. The large stage had been the setting for the Ziegfeld Follies, Sarah Bernhardt, jazz groups, and many other entertainers. The opera house was built in the grand days of vaudeville but now hosted live productions by the local theatre company.

After the play, we went to the Belmont for coffee and dessert. I kept meeting people from Abbeville. Everyone was friendly. One person said that she knew I was "from off" but she could not tell by my accent where I was born. I started to laugh about being "from off" but realized she was serious. Her name was Joan Davis, a good friend of Miss Margaret. Joan had been the curator of the South Carolina Governor's Mansion and was in Abbeville to promote tourism. She told me she was going to the lake for Margaret's party on Saturday.

Joan informed me that Abbeville was in a historical corridor that covered the area starting above Clemson, extending to Aiken, and on to Charleston. She told me she often stayed at Miss Margaret's house while working in that area. She was an attractive, tall lady with a smooth Southern accent. For some unknown reason, she asked if I was looking to buy a house. I assured her I was not and that I would only be in South Carolina for a year of study. She asked me where I was studying. I said, "Erskine." She commented that Erskine was so convenient, since the school was only twelve miles away.

I called Jack and Evelyn over to meet Joan. We then went to the main dining room for dessert. Afterward, Jack, Evelyn, and I excused ourselves and walked down the hotel front steps and out to the town square. We talked about the heat, but my mind was flooded by thoughts of my late wife's comments about the Abbeville square. Laura thought it was such a perfect place to walk, relax, and forget the hectic world outside. She and I had stayed at the Belmont Inn several times in the mid-1980s. Each time she stated that she felt refreshed by the beauty of the town. The old hotel had a simple elegance she enjoyed. As we walked around the square, I told Jack and Evelyn about Miss Sallie's comment about Miss Margaret "directing people." We laughed and joked about the situation. Jack said he had noticed that trait when Margaret helped with the plays at the opera house.

I drove back to Bowie Hall after the walk, played with Sugar Baby, and checked on the other dogs at the house. I went to bed reflecting on the events of a full day.

Abbeville Opera House

5

The fall of the year arrived with colorful trees and relentless heat. On the last Sunday night in September, the Spaghetti Club met at the home of a lady named Jo Ann. I was invited by several friends of Miss Margaret. Upon arrival at the party, I noticed a group of mixed social classes. We did not eat until about ten o'clock. The drinks lasted a long time. A local waiter helped serve the older ladies. Everyone was welcoming. One man asked me if I had been bitten by Possum. I told him I had not. He laughed and told me a story about the dog biting the Episcopal rector's wife on the ankle. I told him Possum seemed like a happy dog. He told me I could ask Ann Clarke for details.

The spaghetti, salad, and bread were finally served. I met a lady who worked as a missionary and social worker in Central America. She related several stories about her college days in the late 1920s. She said she and Miss Margaret had smoked cigarettes on the back balcony of Winthrop College for Women. Of course, it was forbidden at the time. I met Ruth and George Settles and Myra Keith. They welcomed me to Abbeville. George said Miss Margaret had been instrumental in getting the opera house restored.

The Spaghetti Club was a festive event. Miss Margaret asked me to drive her home even though she had driven to the party. On the way home, Miss Margaret told me how George used to make her house the gathering spot after opening nights. She stated that she never knew when he was going to invite the cast and patrons to come over to Bowie Hall, but she was delighted to have the opera house succeed.

As the fall progressed, school took most of my time. I rarely saw Miss Margaret.

Her son Bill had a serious stroke. He was transferred to Roper Hospital in Charleston, a four-hour drive from Abbeville, where he went into rehabilitation.

I was very busy with my studies and meeting new people at the college. Several of my professors asked me to visit churches in the area, so I went to Lower Long Cane, Troy, and Cedar Springs churches. These churches were old, beautiful, and well preserved. Several times that fall, I took Sugar Baby down to Lower Long Cane. She ran around in the ancient graveyard while I sat on the columned porch of the church. It was peaceful there. I would read a series of the Psalms and meditate. My dog loved the exercise, and I felt renewed.

The fall leaves were outstanding. The heat had begun to lessen so that one could feel a cool breeze at night. Late one afternoon as I was studying I realized that someone was in the house. I walked through the dining room into the breakfast room. I saw that the gate to the enclosed back driveway was open. I remembered I had closed it when I came in from school earlier. I felt that someone was in the downstairs bedroom. As I headed that way, Miss Margaret came out of the back hall to the kitchen. She looked stressed. She smiled with a strained look and greeted me. I sensed something was not right, so I asked her about Bill's health.

As we stood in the kitchen, Miss Margaret said that her son's recovery was questionable. She wondered if he would ever walk again. To my surprise, she asked me what I thought. Before I could answer, she said that she was accustomed to taking care of people, especially her men, but she was concerned that he would never recover from his stroke. She was silent. When I did not speak on the subject as quickly as she expected, she asked again. I told her although she was power-less over his progress, she was a wonderful mother to take such good care of him. She waited for me to continue. I told her I knew she was a very capable person, but she would have to turn Bill's recovery over to God. He had the power over Bill's health and life. She smiled weakly, said nothing, and then turned to walk back into her bedroom. Before I could leave the kitchen, she turned around and added that she had to get back to Charleston. Her tone had changed. She said she hoped I was enjoying Abbeville. Then she thanked me for taking care of the dogs and the house. She stood there for a minute as if she was thinking and then said, "No one ever suggested to turn over concerns to God." She then abruptly turned and walked away, leaving me to wonder how she took my suggestion.

6

The month of December arrived, but the days continued to be warm. I relaxed a little about school and found myself enjoying the old house on Greenville Street. My dog, Sugar Baby, had settled down also.

One morning while eating breakfast, I noticed that Possum was climbing over the six-foot wall surrounding the backyard. The iron gate at the driveway entrance was closed, but the dog simply put one paw on the bottom stone and climbed up the wall. I had heard the gardener say that Possum was part wild dog. As she reached the top of the wall, she stopped a minute and surveyed the surrounding driveway and the two neighboring yards. After a brief time atop the wall, Possum jumped down and was gone. I wondered if the dog was a cross between a small wolf and a collie. I had heard that Possum had breakfast fairly often at a home on Chestnut Street.

Miss Margaret and her son Bill came home from Charleston in the second week of December. He was weak but able to walk.

He would continue his recovery at Bowie Hall. Miss Margaret's downstairs bedroom held two large four-poster antique beds. She slept in one while Bill slept in the other bed. They had an argument about how he was going to get onto the bed, which was at least four feet off the floor. After words were exchanged, she walked upstairs and got the wooden steps from what she called her mother's bed. Bill refused to climb the steps to get into the poster bed. Miss Margaret went to the dining room and poured herself a glass of sherry from the decanter. After drinking the sherry, she declared that Bill could never live at the lake unless he cooperated with her. He replied that he was sure he would fall out of bed. She assured him that she was going to watch over him and would put pillows all around to keep him in the bed. Bill settled down and stayed through the Christmas holidays. He then moved to the house on Lake Secession with his dog.

The Belmont Inn

On the third Sunday in December, Miss Margaret had a small Christmas luncheon at the Belmont Inn downtown. She invited me and about twelve other people. The hotel was decorated with holiday greenery. Margaret's reserved tables had silver bowls filled with red carnations and holly. I sat next to Reverend Clarke, the rector at Trinity Church in Abbeville, and his wife Ann. Misses Ella and Sallie McMillan were there with others. Miss Ada Allen was joined by a cousin from Savannah. Miss Margaret sat at the head of the table. All were dressed in their finery. When I think back on these occasions, I wonder how many oysters must have sacrificed their pearls to drape around the beautiful necks of Southern women.

After dessert was served, Miss Margaret announced that she was not going to have her Christmas open house this year, saying that

Bill's illness was the reason. Everyone agreed with the rector, who reassured her that all understood what a difficult fall it had been.

After lunch, I decided to walk back to Bowie Hall. I exited the main entrance to the hotel and encountered Miss Ella and Miss Sara Milford on the steps of the hotel having a serious conversation. I tried to step to the side, but they turned as if to include me. Miss Ella said in a whisper, "You know, it is better not to have the open house." I was not sure what she was saying so I asked why. She responded by saying Margaret invited only people from old South Carolina families or "refined" newcomers who made their mark on the world. I asked, "Who does that leave out?" In her very sweet voice, Miss Sara responded, "That leaves out those born to mill families or any Yankee Margaret did not like or think was up to her standard of refinement." She then asked me to never mention our conversation to Miss Margaret. I then said, "Good day!" and walked around the square.

The Christmas tree in the square was decorated in all colors with red-and-green roping on the large urns surrounding it. The monument in the center of the square was chipped and rough looking from last year's fire, I had been told. The Christmas tree had been placed over the monument for many years in the past. When the tree caught fire last year, the local firemen poured water onto the tree. The marble monument cracked and chipped. I was told it would be repaired. The decorated square and the embellished stores looked like a town at Christmas in 1860.

When I reached the north end, this impression was briefly broken when I saw the midcentury modern Belk department store. When I looked to my right, there was a quaint bookstore on the corner and the interesting and historic Poliakoff's Department Store across the square. I looked down Trinity Street to see the fine Gothic church at the end. Some of the stores had tin-roofed porches, giving them an antique impression.

I walked up North Main past three churches. On the left side of the street was the splendid Queen Anne-style McGowan-Barksdale-Bundy House. The handsome tower gave the house an appearance of a small wooden castle. The asymmetrical front garden was a little overgrown, which imparted an exotic look. I turned in front of the Burt-Stark Mansion. Greenville Street looked festive, as each house was decorated.

In the Jefferson Davis Park I could see Possum. The dog began to follow me. I hoped she was not in a biting mood. She wagged her tail the entire time as we walked up the street. Possum and I had our first real talk as we stood on the porch of Bowie Hall. I felt a little more at ease around the dog, so I patted her on the head. She wagged her tail. She then moved behind me to sit down in front of the door, taking a guard dog position. I opened the door quickly and stepped inside. As I closed the door, Possum sat down before the door and looked toward the street. I watched this unusual dog for a moment.

Christmas was the time of year when Miss Margaret had found her on the square. Possum had had four puppies several days later on Christmas Day.

When I turned around, I realized someone had put up a Christmas tree in the entrance hall in front of the grandfather clock. A woman came out of the dining room and introduced herself as a local florist. I complimented her on the beautiful tree and her expertise. Then I excused myself and quickly went to get Sugar Baby for her daily walk. As we passed through the den, I could hear Miss Margaret on the phone, saying that she opposed something, and the ladies would organize to stop it. She lowered her voice as we passed through the room. I waved and went out the back door. The metal carriage gate was open, so Sugar Baby and I walked down to the street. The afternoon seemed unseasonably warm. Sugar Baby stopped at one point and wanted me to fix her collar that had gotten twisted. I patted her. Then we walked down Greenville Street to Jefferson Davis Park.

I sat on a bench and thought about Christmas in Tennessee, while Sugar Baby explored the grass, the bugs, and the park. In a while, we walked back to Bowie Hall. Possum was still sitting outside the front door. We walked up the front steps and onto the porch, but Possum did not seem to notice. Rather than make Possum move, we went in the back door.

Possum in front of Bowie Hall

7

That night, I went to the home of Reverend and Mrs. Clarke for dinner. I walked two blocks to their house on Chestnut Street. I had met the two of them at a summer camp in western North Carolina in 1991, the year after my wife Laura died. Both of them were warm, outgoing people who often opened their home for social events and prayer groups. Though I did not know them well, I could sense the mixture of Southern refinement and a sense of humor. They had that wonderful warmth that comes from enjoying people and the celebration of a good time. They greeted me and invited me into a large hall that ran through the center of the house.

Inside, the ceiling must have been fourteen feet high. On the right side of the hall was a large parlor with an ornate carved Eastlake fireplace. Two light blue wing chairs flanked the fireplace, and a small sofa was placed on the wall opposite the entrance to the room. Two large oriental porcelain vases stood on either side of the fireplace. A large bay window gave the room a spacious feeling. I was offered a seat and a glass of sherry. As I sat down, I noticed the massive doors leading into the room. On the other side of the wide hall was a dining room with a table and an old Sheraton sideboard. Above the sideboard was a large painting of a clipper ship that carried cargo to America. The Clarke family had owned the ship at one time.

We sat in the parlor and talked about the day's events. Of course, one of the first topics was the perennially great Abbeville High School football team. Phil was quite enthusiastic and informed us all about the players—positive and negative. Miss Margaret had informed me that Ann and Phil had "background," which I had come to realize meant "a refined way of conducting oneself."

Ann went into the kitchen several times. She explained that she did not grow up cooking but had learned how to as a minister's wife. She said that when the mills opened in the 1960s, everyone had to adjust to doing their own work. It had been good for everyone. I wondered if others shared her opinion.

We went into the dining room for a wonderful dinner of shrimp and grits. As we ate, they asked me if I liked living in Abbeville. However, before I could answer, they talked about how small towns in South Carolina are like small city-states, each with its own history, politics, and character! I finally broke in and stated that I liked the slow pace, the nice people, and the beautiful trees and architecture.

Ann said they had lived in Charleston and four other small towns. She then paused and looked at Phil. I waited as they continued to look at each other. Finally, Phil said, "Gossip is an art form here." Ann stated that usually some fact or event was interpreted in the wrong way or given a dark interpretation. He added that often Miss Margaret was the topic of gossip since she was a town leader and so outspoken. He went on the say that many were afraid of her because she had "gotten so many people told." Ann said that she loved Miss Margaret, but that she was quite bold and direct in her words. She went on to say that when Possum bit her and their wonderful gardener, Margaret blamed them for irritating the dog. Ann followed her declaration of being bitten with an apology for getting off the subject of gossip.

We all agreed that I was probably already being talked about as Miss Margaret's renter. We laughed and agreed that the fallen nature of man is everywhere, even in beautiful old Abbeville. Ann asked that we go into the living room for coffee, and I thanked her for a wonderful dinner and dessert.

Phil asked if I had been bitten yet. I said I hoped that Possum and I had become friends, but I wondered about that now. Phil said that he and Ann wanted me to know the events following Ann and the gardener getting bitten. He stated that when Margaret realized that that the gardener had indeed been bitten, she insisted that he go to the ER to be checked out. Phil said he took the gardener. Margaret called the hospital to check on him and assure the hospital she would pay for his visit. That afternoon, she called Phil to say that she would pay for the visit. She was sorry it happened, but there must be a reason Possum bit him.

After that event, they did not hear from Miss Margaret for about two weeks. She finally called and said she needed to see them at once. She would come for sherry at four that afternoon. She arrived promptly with an intense expression on her face. They welcomed her into the parlor and had a glass of sherry. After one sip, Margaret wanted to know why Ann and the gardener had agitated Possum. She had thought about it a long time, and she realized that Possum was by nature a guard dog and would not normally bite them. She asked in a forceful voice, "The dog is such a sweet dog. Why did you agitate Possum?" Ann said they both wanted to laugh out loud but realized how serious she was. "We tried to assure Margaret that we had not irritated the dog or provoked her. She stood her ground. Finally, she declared that she had to go to the town city council meeting. We hugged and said good-bye. We laughed so hard after she left." Phil declared that denial will blind every time, especially when it is about a dog. He said he learned that day that Margaret Bowie was not going to admit that Possum ever bit an innocent person or dog.

I was a little surprised by this story and decided not to make any comment. We laughed and ended my visit by talking again about the outstanding Abbeville football team.

As I walked up Chestnut Street to Greenville Street, I thought back to the morning in June 1993 when I called Ann Clarke to inquire about a room to rent in Abbeville. She told me that the night before, she had a dream that I would call. I sensed at that time her dream was one of those mysterious affirmations, a sign to move forward! She confirmed the sign several days later with a follow-up letter telling me about a room at Bowie Hall. I pondered the wonderful evening, great dinner, and celebration of life with new friends.

A series of open doors had led me to the Clarkes, to Miss Margaret and Bowie Hall, and to graduate school. My South Carolina adventure had fallen into place. Tonight, I was not going to think about

Abbeville gossip or Miss Margaret's denial. I was going to celebrate the wonderful evening and good times with new friends. I arrived back at Bowie Hall. Thank goodness Possum was not guarding the front door. She must have been out roaming the town.

8

After passing finals, I returned to Knoxville and enjoyed Christmas with my family. Sugar Baby and I returned to Abbeville on a Saturday to get ready for the school term in January. That Sunday, I joined Misses Margaret, Ella, and others at the Belmont Inn for brunch. Miss Ella was talking about her Perrin ancestors when Miss Margaret turned to her and asked her to change the subject. Miss Ella raised her voice and said, "But, Margaret, they were important!" Miss Margaret returned to the conversation and said that all South Carolinians ate rice and worshiped their ancestors, but she (Miss Ella) was extreme with it. Margaret lowered her voice and said that Ella was so Southern that she kissed the magnolia trees in her front yard, and she had seen Ella do it.

Miss Ella offered a faint smile and asked everyone if they wanted dessert and then excused herself. She said she had to talk to Mr. Puff and she would return soon. "Seeing Mr. Puff" was her code for wanting to smoke. It took me a while to realize she smoked, but I should have guessed it since she was so thin. After Miss Ella left, Miss Margaret said she knew Ella had a PhD in English but sometimes she did not know what to do with her. Miss Ada, who was Miss Margaret's equal in the use of Southern English language, announced to Miss Margaret that she sure hoped she realized that Miss Ella was a force in keeping the Burt-Stark Mansion. Miss Margaret agreed, and everyone went into the hall for dessert. Miss Ella returned, smelling of cigarette smoke after having her time with Mr. Puff.

Graduate school became more difficult, so I studied more. When I would go to the library, Miss Margaret let my dog come into her den or go outside with Possum and Daisy, Possum's daughter. They had a great time playing outside together. When Possum got tired of the two younger dogs, she would scale the six-foot wall and be gone.

One night, I was studying late in my room when I saw a police car flashing its light pull into the driveway. I walked into the living room and into the front hall. Miss Margaret was heading to the front door. She said that the alarm was going off at the Burt-Stark Mansion, so the police were taking her to investigate. She said most likely Possum had been locked up in the mansion by one of the tour guides. I learned later that Possum would sometimes sleep on the beds during the tours. If she was not ready to leave, she would hide under a bed. When the guides closed up, she would come out or wait to leave in the middle of the night. That night, she was ready to leave at eleven. (It is interesting to note that Possum got a bath about twice a year, so the beds were being slept on by a not-so-clean dog.)

When people came for the tour, everyone with tennis shoes had to take them off. They were told that tennis shoes cut up the carpets in the house. When asked a second time why they had to take off their shoes, the guides, on instruction from Misses Ella and Margaret, replied, "A new study showed that the edge of a tennis shoe sole was almost as sharp as a knife, so please take off your tennis shoes."

One day, I saw Miss Ella's niece Margaret Perrin downtown. I knew she had volunteered as a guide at the mansion. I asked her if anyone ever said anything about Possum sleeping on the beds. She had invited me to a dinner party at her house several months before, so I thought maybe she would give me some insight. She looked straight at me and stated, "No one is willing to take on that battle. As long as Ella and Margaret are around, that dog is going to sleep anywhere she wants!"

We laughed. I told her again what a beautiful party she had. I asked her about her guide duties at the mansion. I joked that since she was a Perrin, she would be in charge one day. Her voice took on a serious tone when she said, "You know, I have the pedigree as a Perrin, the education, and the background to be there, but after one day with those two old ladies, I had the worst headache I ever had.

They kept telling me that I was doing okay with the tours, but I was not walking up and down the stairs in a proper manner." She said that she wanted to do her duty, but she had never had headaches before, so she was not doing tours. I said I was sorry it had not turned out so well. She replied that she was sorry too, and that we all needed to get together again for another dinner party.

As school progressed, some of us developed a study group. We would get together in Tim Erskine's room at the seminary. He had a new computer that organized material, so he was able to print everyone a study copy.

In April of that year, I returned to Bowie Hall after my study group. Miss Margaret and I almost ran into each other in the kitchen. She stated that she was going to Ruth Harris' home to a meeting for planning the president's visit. I asked her if President Clinton was coming to Abbeville. She seemed a little upset and stated that May 2 would be the anniversary of the visit of Jefferson Davis in 1865 and the end of the War for Southern Independence. She quickly stated that she would tell me later and vanished out the back door. I noted for her on May 2 of each year, the "president" was Jefferson Davis. I did not need to make that mistake again!

I knew that she was really smart and in touch with reality. Her broker Marc Dobbs called her regularly. She had been very successful as a house and subdivision developer in the sixties to eighties, and the state had installed her as the head of the Burt-Stark Mansion. It occurred to me that the ladies were trying to preserve a time and place that was historic and genteel. I had not seen anyone love their town and history so much as these ladies. They were far from perfect, but I admired their determination and commitment to Abbeville.

Spring arrived in Abbeville. The dogwoods and tulips were outstanding. The downtown square was manicured, and new flowers filled the urns and beds. The large leafy trees provided a canopy over the square.

Miss Margaret organized a tour of old houses for my visitors from Tennessee. After the tour, she would serve sherry in her large antique-filled parlor. She would tell stories of weddings, parties, and ghosts at the various places. She loved to elaborate about the 1898 wedding in Cedar Springs at the Frazier-Pressley Mansion. Her husband's aunts were in the wedding. She described the two grand staircases in the house and the reception afterward. She would describe the carriages and horses that transported the wedding party.

She pointed out that Miss Ella's house and other houses had magnolia trees planted right up to the edge of the foundations to provide shade from the South Carolina sun as well as for protection during storms.

Often a guest would ask Margaret about the beautiful layout of the town. She would explain that Robert Mills, the famous South Carolina architect, and his wife Eliza had lived in a yellow cottage on North Main Street.

Miss Margaret was told as a child that Mills influenced the design of the town. He designed the third courthouse and the old jail. Margaret related that the Mills cottage had been on the site of a present-day Catholic church. Mr. Burt was helpful in getting Robert Mills the commission to design the Washington Monument in the nation's capital and gave Mills the money to get settled in Washington, DC. Mrs. Mills stayed behind for a short time in the lovely yellow cottage. Mr. Burt acted as her gentleman protector. Everyone enjoyed their visit to Bowie Hall.

The first year at Erskine College was coming to an end. I enjoyed the study. Several churches had opened up for me to serve them. After consulting with Dean Randy Ruble, I decided to take a second year and finish the degree program by taking Greek.

9

Tim and I agreed to work at the Burt-Stark Mansion during the summer as tour guides and take classes each morning. One week into the schedule of tours, Miss Margaret asked me to swap schedules with Tim so I could take her to pick up an unexpected visitor from Arizona. As we drove to the Greenville airport, Miss Margaret told me that the woman from Arizona would be staying with her for a week or two. She did not really know her, but she was taking her in because her host, Mrs. Furman, needed to go out of town.

The day turned out to be a stormy afternoon. When the plane landed, we picked up the guest. On meeting the woman, I noticed Miss Margaret looking at the shell bracelet of the guest. She asked if the bracelet made that much noise all the time. The woman did not respond to Miss Margaret's question but thanked her for picking her up and letting her stay at her home. She was an attractive person in her forties with blonde hair. She was dressed in a white pantsuit and was carrying a bag of gifts. They sat in the back of Miss Margaret's white Cadillac. I concentrated on driving, since the rainstorm was quite heavy with a lot of lightning. Miss Margaret and her guest talked about Arizona and South Carolina.

Upon arriving at Bowie Hall, I unpacked the car and took the luggage upstairs to one of the two large guest rooms. Miss Margaret had prepared the east bedroom for her. The room had a large four-poster bed with steps to get up to it. The marble-topped table next to the bed held a vase of fresh flowers. The room was almost cold, even for summer. The twelve-foot ceiling made the room look larger than it was.

The guest and Miss Margaret sat in the back den. I went to my room to study. Then I checked the front door to make sure it was locked before I went to bed. When I went to lock the door, I heard Miss Margaret getting another bottle of sherry out of the cabinet in the breakfast room. Sherry hospitality was very important at Bowie Hall.

At about three o'clock in the morning, I was awakened by some-one coming down the steps at a fast pace. I put on my robe and went into the front hall. I could see a light in the breakfast room behind the dining room. As I walked to the breakfast room, our guest Pat was sitting on the corner chair. She had her robe pulled up around her neck and was shaking all over. I asked her what was wrong. She looked wild-eyed and afraid. She just shook her head. I offered her a glass of water, which she refused. I went into the kitchen and got a glass for myself. I thought maybe I should call Miss Margaret. After a while, she cleared her throat and asked about a big black bug that she saw on the ceiling in her room. She did not realize South Carolina had such large bugs. I told her that the palmetto bug was common here, but the netting over her bed would keep one from falling on her. She seemed skeptical and asked me if the bugs bit. I responded that if one did bite her, the wound would not be fatal. She turned pale and became silent. Before I left, I tried to reassure her that I never heard of anyone being bitten, but I was from Tennessee where we do not have such bugs. I started to go into the rat problem but decided to avoid the topic. I added that Miss Margaret had the house sprayed last winter for bugs and rats after a large rat walked through the den as Miss Margaret watched the six o'clock news. Before I left, I tried to convince her that the bugs were not dangerous. She sat frozen in the breakfast room, so I excused myself and went back to my room.

The next day was clear. The sky was blue and the sun bright, but a cold breeze assured me that it was spring in Abbeville. I got up for an early class. Later that day, Miss Margaret toured her guest around the town. That night, they ate at the Village Grill with some other people. I assumed that our guest had adjusted to the bugs, since all was peaceful through the night. I left the house the next morning for my early class. Miss Margaret was in the kitchen making toast when I walked through the back of the house. She related that she and Pat were having a pleasant time. Miss Margaret said that our guest was a good conversationalist.

I returned from class around twelve-thirty and entered the house through the front door. Much to my surprise, Miss Margaret was sitting in the entrance hall on a small Victorian side chair next to the grandfather clock. As soon as I entered, she stood up and stated somberly that she was waiting for her houseguest. She had two disturbing phone calls from friends that morning. Both ladies had seen our houseguest walking downtown toward the square. This situation was not any of my business, so I excused myself. As I was turning to go into my room, I saw Pat standing at the front door. She seemed surprised when Miss Margaret opened the door. I quickly walked to my room. I knew I did not want to be present to witness the coming event. However, since my room was in the old sunroom right off the entrance hall, I heard every word of the confrontation.

In a raised voice, Miss Margaret asked Pat if she walked downtown dressed in the outfit she was wearing. Pat replied that she did. "And what's wrong with that?" Miss Margaret stated she was not going to have any guest in her house "parade herself" downtown in such a revealing costume. It was not proper for her to parade herself around in shorts and a halter covered only by a thin lace jacket. After a short silence, Pat raised her voice and stated that she wore this outfit in Arizona all the time. Miss Margaret quickly replied that Abbeville was not Arizona, and that Pat was not going to parade herself in such a skimpy costume. Pat argued, telling Miss Margaret that she was not going to be told what to do or how to dress. Miss Margaret replied that she would never tell anyone what to do. It was not her habit to tell people what to do! Then there was silence. As Pat walked up the stairs, I could hear Miss Margaret saying, "This is Abbeville, and there is a standard here. I am going to maintain that standard!" All went silent.

Reconciliation must have taken place because Miss Margaret and Pat drove out to the farm on the lake. Miss Margaret told me how she had Winn-Dixie fix them a picnic so they could enjoy the lake house. She also wanted to see the progress on the new addition to the farm. When they arrived, the workers were still present, and there was a problem with some of the hardware for the doors and windows. The foreman asked Miss Margaret to go to town and get the hardware so they could continue working early the next morning. She returned to town. Pat asked to stay so she could enjoy the lake.

When Miss Margaret returned, Pat and one of the men were talking down by the lake. Miss Margaret inspected the job, then she and Pat returned to town. As they got out of the car, Pat informed Miss Margaret that she had a date that night and asked if she could have a key to the back door because Possum was at the front door, and she was afraid of the dog. She gave Pat a key and wished her a good time.

The next day, Pat told Miss Margaret that she had enjoyed the lake so much, she had rented a trailer there. She would be moving out that afternoon. Miss Margaret said she was so shocked that there was no sherry time with Pat that afternoon.

In the following weeks, there were many comments from the ladies of Abbeville. Miss Sallie said that apparently Pat did not come to Abbeville for the history. Miss Ella told everyone Pat must have wanted to get away from the black bugs at Margaret's house. Miss Margaret said she agreed with Ella that the move was about a different type of bug, not the Abbeville black bugs.

When Pat's sponsor returned to town the next week, Miss Margaret explained to her that Pat had moved to the lake. The lady denied knowing her, except they had worked together in Atlanta years ago. She praised Miss Margaret for being "so sweet" to Pat.

A local merchant, Mr Blackwell, said he thought Pat and Jefferson Davis had a great deal in common since each one had slept one night in a historic house and then escaped just in time not to be bored. Two of the ladies said they were going to boycott his store on Trinity Street, but Miss Ada reminded them that he mostly sold used furniture. None of them was buying furniture, especially secondhand things! Mr. Blackwell told me the women should celebrate, since President Davis and Pat had so much in common. We laughed.

10

The semester ended. Summer seemed to arrive early when the hot weather showed up in Abbeville. Miss Margaret took me to lunch at the Belmont Inn the day before I left for Tennessee. While we were eating, Misses Ada and Sallie came in and joined us. Miss Ada said she remembered the wild debutante parties they had in the 1920s and 1930s. Miss Margaret broke in and said they stopped all that wild stuff. Miss Sallie stated that they organized a women's group and brought about many good changes. Miss Margaret said that they made a difference. "Those men thought they were going to run things, but we brought some class and refinement to those events." I felt as though I was invisible when Miss Ada said that women had made a big difference in Abbeville in every way. Miss Sallie stated, "Nowadays, it is called 'women's lib,' but we have always had it here. We called it 'steel magnolia.'" Finally, they changed the subject and asked me about my plans for the summer. They obviously were not telling me some things! Miss Ada told me she and Margaret were 1920s flappers. I would like to have seen that.

The next day, I packed up. I noticed Possum sat at the front door and did not come to the back courtyard to see us off. Sugar Baby and I drove five hours over the mountains to Tennessee.

The summer passed quickly as I worked at the First Presbyterian Church in Knoxville, visiting shut-ins and making hospital visits. Counseling individuals and couples was also part of the work. It was good to be in the green hills of Tennessee where the air was refreshed most afternoons by the summer showers. My relatives fed me chicken, green beans, potato salad and biscuits so I was nourished in every way. I felt ready for my second year of graduate school at Erskine when I returned to Abbeville. Though my sweet mother insisted that I was unstable for doing graduate work at my advanced age of fifty years, I felt the way was open to finish the degree.

Miss Margaret was staying at her lake house during the first week of my return. Possum and Daisy welcomed us back. Tim Erskine came by and said he enjoyed working as a tour guide at the Burt-Stark Mansion that summer. He stated that Senator Strom Thurmond had been at the mansion for a promotional event, Possum had been in and out of the mansion as she pleased, and Miss Margaret knew the placement of every book in the Burt-Stark Mansion. He went on to tell me that he borrowed a book about General Lee from the bookcase one afternoon and took it home. The next morning, Miss Margaret asked him if he had the book or if someone had stolen it. When he told her he borrowed it, she was relieved and told him to enjoy it but to bring it back. He said that he could not believe how smart she was. "She is amazing! She can really raise money for the mansion," he said.

To redirect our conversation, I asked Tim if he had seen any ghosts. I did not expect any serious response, but he said that Miss Margaret told him about Mr. Kerr, the ghost. Mr. Kerr was the first husband of Fanny Stark, one of the sisters who donated the mansion to the state of South Carolina. Tim said that he got a call one night from Miss Margaret that someone had left the lights on at the mansion. He said that he had checked everything before he left that afternoon. Miss Margaret went up to the mansion with Possum at her side. Once inside the entrance hall, Possum refused to go up the stairs, so she left the lights on. She explained that several times in her tenure as board president she thought that Mr. Kerr or something showed up at the mansion. She said she was happy to leave him alone. I learned later that Mr. Kerr died mysteriously in the front upstairs bedroom. His death left Fanny a widow until she married Mr. Connor from Orangeburg a few years later.

Tim and I decided that Miss Margaret did not really think there was a ghost, but the tale made for a good story for visitors. I asked him if he told the tourists about Mr. Kerr's ghost. He said no. He thought Miss Ella focused on the tragic Miss Fanny, who suffered so much until she married Mr. Connor, her first sweetheart. We decided to let it all go, as this saga was a part of Abbeville history.

I was facing a year of graduate study which would include a year of Greek. I thought that solving the mystery of Mr. Kerr might have been harder to figure out than learning Greek. When I tried to find out details about Mr. Kerr from some of the ladies, they changed the subject and wanted to talk about the old carpet that Tim Erskine found under newer carpets at the mansion. The Brussels carpets were colorful machine-made European floor coverings that were fashionable in the first half of the nineteenth century. Apparently, Tim was quite the hero, since he found the original carpet that Jefferson Davis had walked on.

11

Miss Margaret came home from the lake and asked me to go to the grocery store with her. She said she needed to restock the pantry. We had a brief conversation about the summer. We got into her Cadillac and drove up North Main Street to the Winn-Dixie. She asked me about my work at the church and my family. She said it had been a big benefit to her to have Tim work at the mansion. As we drove up North Main, several people waved, but Miss Margaret kept her eyes on the road. Once she nodded to a man who she said worked for their family business.

I noticed one automobile pulled to the side of the road as we arrived at Winn-Dixie on North Main. She drove right up to the front door. I told her she had parked in the fire lane. She turned to me and said very firmly, "No one ever questioned me, and no one will today!" After she filled a cart full and paid for the groceries, a young man loaded them in the car. Much to my surprise, no one said anything about her parking. The only words she heard were "Good morning, Miss Margaret!" and "Thank you, Miss Margaret." She had given the young man at Winn-Dixie a nice tip.

Several days later, I saw Miss Sara downtown and asked her if other ladies parked in the fire lane. Miss Sara's husband had worked for Mr. Bowie's company. Even though the heat was oppressive, I needed to find out about the parking. Miss Sara said that she did not park in the fire lane. She stated: "People are afraid of Margaret!" She was genteel and reserved, so I knew I was getting the truth.

As fall progressed, the heat lessened and the autumn leaves turned especially colorful. The graduate school classes were more difficult, so a group of us studied together. One night, two of the men dropped by Bowie Hall to study. Miss Margaret was in the breakfast room, putting up some glasses. When the students entered, she offered them a glass of sherry, which was her custom. After being introduced to the men, she realized that one of them was from the North. She offered him a glass of wine. Not realizing she was going to pour him a full glass, he picked up a large iced tea glass and handed it to her. She filled it with red wine. The other student, Tim, received a small glass of sherry. Everyone thanked her and then went into the parlor to study. She told them that if anyone needed a room to stay for the night, they could come to her house. She especially liked the Yankee who drank his wine out of an iced tea glass. Since three empty bedrooms were available at Bowie Hall, they were often in use by students. The next day, she told me that she had not thought she would like Erskine students, but she had found them fun and humorous. She said that she could not believe that Richard the Yankee drank his wine out of an iced tea glass.

While studying at Erskine, I worked at two churches down from Abbeville, Troy and Lower Long Cane. At one of the churches, the head elder had cancer. I would visit Mr. Young often. He was a very thin man in his eighties. As I entered his room, he would sit up on an antique daybed. After a short time, he had to lie back down. He liked to talk about the church and the old times, specifically an old sword that his ancestor used in the War for Southern Independence. I visited Mr. Young many times that fall. During one visit, he told me about his ancestor who saw Jefferson Davis arriving at the ferry on the Savannah River in 1865. How busy that day must have been. After our time together, I read him a psalm, and we prayed together. He patted my hand. Mrs. Young came in as I was leaving and thanked me. I sensed that they knew where they were going with the illness, and yet all was well. They seemed grateful for the visits.

Miss Margaret often asked me about my days at the church. I told her about visiting Mr. Young and others in nursing homes. She asked in frustration how visiting the sick people was helping the church. Her husband had been ill for a long time, and no one ever came to visit him. I wondered if the minister was afraid to visit, but I did not say it aloud. Usually, I would say something about loving the people or it was my duty. It made no sense to her to drive twenty-five or thirty miles to visit people who would never come to church. I explained that my repeated visits were about showing love.

12

In late October, the weather turned rainy and cold. I decided to pick up an early lunch for us at the Dutch Oven restaurant. As I was walking up the sidewalk, I ran into Misses Ella and Sara. Miss Ella took me by the arm and said she was worried she would never get a doctor in Abbeville after what happened at the Mansion. We all went inside and sat down at a back table. She told me that she and Miss Margaret had been on duty at the Mansion when three teenagers showed up for a tour.

The teens came in the entrance hall. Miss Margaret asked them why they were there. They seemed puzzled by the question. They said their mother had dropped them off to do research for some paper they had to write. Miss Ella said about that time she heard Possum at the front door. As everyone stood in the entrance hall, Miss Margaret opened the door and let Possum in the room. Then she led the dog into the back hall to find a place to rest. When Miss Margaret came back into the room, she asked the teens to sit on the porch until their mother returned. She added, "Please come back for a tour" when they had an idea what their paper was about. Nothing was said about their tennis shoes cutting up the carpets.

Miss Ella said that the weather was cool that day, but sunny when this happened. Miss Ella said that she and Miss Margaret were working on some paperwork for the Mansion. Suddenly, there was a knocking on the door by someone who really knew how to use a brass knocker. Miss Margaret stood up from the table and announced she would "manage the situation." Miss Margaret walked slowly to the door as the knocking increased, with Miss Ella following her. Miss

Margaret slowly opened the door and said, "Good afternoon. May I help you?"

A well-dressed woman stated that she did not like it that her children did not get a tour and certainly did not like it that they had to sit on the porch in the cool weather. Miss Ella related that Miss Margaret stepped forward and informed the woman that she had not prepared her children for their visit to the Mansion, so a tour would not have worked for them. The woman made some comment that Miss Ella did not hear, but she did hear Miss Margaret say that she had not done her job as their mother. The woman was obviously a little surprised, but she quickly recovered her composure and raised her voice to say, "Do you know who I am?" Miss Margaret calmly said that she did not. The woman stood squarely as if she were throwing the final blow in a boxing match. "I am the wife of the new doctor in town." Miss Margaret leaned backward as if to brace herself. She then told the woman, "Lady, I don't care whose new doctor's wife you are! Good day to you!" She then closed the large door as the woman stood there in amazement.

Miss Ella said that she stood in the hall until Miss Margaret said that they needed to finish their paperwork. There was not another knock at the door until four in the afternoon when a scheduled tour group arrived. After hearing about the confrontation, I wanted to reassure Miss Ella that no one knew she was there, so she could see the doctor if she needed. I laughed to myself. I was sure I would not hear this story from Miss Margaret.

School took much of my time that fall. Many a Friday night, I would meet Jack and Evelyn at the Grill, and then we would walk around the beautiful square. Sometimes Miss Margaret would join us. We hadn't heard about the doctor's wife, but we did hear about the Christmas tree auction sponsored by the hospice foundation in Greenwood. In the old South, true ladies never went to an auction, so the ladies of the Mansion did not want the name of Misses Fanny and Mary connected to the Hospice Christmas Auction. They reasoned that having a tree with their benefactors' names on it would be seen as a disgrace and destroy the ladies' reputations. When I tried to remind Miss Margaret that the ladies had been dead for over ten years, she quickly told me that that did not matter. I guess it was one of those "shadows" of the old South. She stated that the entire matter was under control because she and two ladies had decided to delay the board meeting, so no vote could be taken before the auction. When I tried to say what good advertisement the hospice auction was, she stopped me midsentence by saying that the ladies who had donated the Burt-Stark Mansion were "private and proper." They would not want their names associated with a "common" tree auction.

We went back to eating. After Miss Margaret left, we discussed the idea that living in Abbeville was like living in a time warp. The year 1860 was still alive, at least in the minds of the Mansion ladies.

Two weeks later, Joan Davis visited Miss Margaret for the weekend. She had worked as a curator at the South Carolina Governor's Mansion. When I asked her about the tree auction, she explained that in the old South, a respectable lady's name was to appear in a newspaper only on four occasions: birth, marriage, death, and proper social events. Business events like tree auctions did not count as "proper." We laughed and talked about the "shadows of gentility" that survived even in our time.

13

On a Sunday afternoon before Christmas, Miss Margaret had her open house. She served ham biscuits, pound cake, fruitcake, red-and-green sugar cookies, and homemade pimento cheese. Featured was the favorite Christmas special drink, Abbeville Gypsy, a milk-and-egg custard flavored with sherry. I was told the recipe had been guarded by families of Abbeville for generations.

The large table in the dining room was set with linen, a cut glass punch bowl, colorful fruit plates, and silver—all giving a soft glow by candles reflecting light through crystal candleholders. The reflection of so much light gave the sense that the room was moving. The setting was quite magical. Champagne was served to adults in the kitchen. The party was festive. All the "people of quality" were there. Miss Margaret greeted guests at the door. Robyn and Paul Agnew were the first to arrive.

I circulated and enjoyed the friendliness of the people. No one asked me if I had been bitten by Possum. After a time, I excused myself to go to Troy Presbyterian Church, one of the churches where I was working. Before I left, I thanked Miss Margaret. As I walked through the dining room, I noticed a large flower arrangement in the center of the table. The display was made of boxwood cuttings and red camellias placed in a silver bowl which stood on a pedestal. The Bowie ancestors looked down from their painted portraits on the wall, the candlelight danced through the crystals, and the smell of boxwood filled the air. I felt I was experiencing a scene from old Abbeville.

Aside from the beautiful setting, these were Miss Margaret's "group," as she called them. Present was a sense of love and harmony among them. They had pulled together to make Abbeville a great village, but they also made me feel that I was a part of a beautiful place and time. I thanked Misses Sara and Sallie for their part of the party.

As I walked down Greenville Street to my car, I thought of the Gypsy I had consumed. It was good. I thought of how much I was enjoying being in Abbeville. Somewhere in my mind, an idea came that I might even "kiss the magnolia tree." I caught myself and did a little rational self-talk. The real world came back into focus. I drove down to be with the youth group at Troy Church.

The Sunday morning before Christmas, I was informed by Miss Margaret that she and Miss Ella were coming to Troy Church. She asked if I would be preaching. I told her I would, and my stomach started turning over as anxiety filled my mind. I drove the twenty-five miles to Troy, praying for relaxation and the ability to lead the celebration of worship. I soon forgot about their attendance. After the service, Misses Ella and Margaret came to the back door where I was greeting the people. Miss Margaret seemed determined to be the last person out. I did not think much about this because many of the people crowded around them to make sure they were greeted. Even in the small village of Troy, these two ladies were well known. Miss Margaret came up to me to thank me and said that she had a strong sense of peace that morning. She shook my hand firmly and went out on the church porch. When I joined the group on the porch, I could hear someone giving Misses Ella and Margaret the directions to the Perrin farm at Hard Labor Creek where Miss Ella's ancestor had lived. They went on their way. I returned to Abbeville to eat lunch at the Belmont Inn with some of the people from Troy Church. The hotel looked festive with the tall Christmas tree in the lobby.

Christmas Eve was on Wednesday of that week. I was busy getting ready for the service that evening. I visited several people who were ill. I planned to go home to Tennessee on Christmas morning to be with my family. Miss Margaret was planning to have a Christmas Eve dessert. A bowl of Gypsy had arrived Christmas Eve morning. By midafternoon, a caterer brought a variety of Christmas cookies and cakes.

I left the house at about three and drove the south to Troy Church. The old wooden church was decorated for Christmas. Mrs. Cox and Mrs. Robinson had a committee that worked hard on the decorations. The poinsettias were grown by the Russell family. As I sat in the beautiful room, a question came to my mind, *Is the Holy Spirit working on Mrs. Bowie's mind and heart?* The musicians, Donna and Pam, came in. We worked on the final details for the service. The Newby family and others filled the church. The service went well. The youth choir was outstanding!

Troy Presbyterian Church

I drove to Greenwood and had dinner with Jack and Evelyn. Then I arrived back at Bowie Hall at around ten-thirty in the evening. Miss Margaret was cleaning up from her dessert party. I entered the front door and noticed the beauty of the room and the red flowers in the middle of the table. Before I could concentrate on the flowers, two words jumped into my consciousness, *Holy Spirit.* I walked into the kitchen where Miss Margaret was washing dishes in the sink. I asked her how the party went. She turned and smiled. She said everyone seemed to enjoy themselves. I offered to help her tidy up. She said I could help pick up the dishes in the dining room and kitchen. I followed her.

As we picked up the silver flatware and dirty dishes, she talked about being disappointed that several people had not been able to attend. I felt a sense of anxiety but also a pulsing sensation in my mind. When we had put the plates on the center counter in the kitchen, I told her that I knew she knew who Jesus Christ was as a person in history, but I wondered if she had ever received Him and His Holy Spirit into her heart. I felt more anxiety but also affirmation as I waited. Within a moment, she said that she had never received Him, but that she needed to. When she reached out her hands to me, I took them. She repeated the words, "I need to." We bowed our heads as I prayed, "On this Christmas Eve, would the God of heaven, the Blesser, give Margaret Bowie Christ and the Holy Spirit in her heart." We stood in silence for a moment. Then she hugged me and smiled. I was overcome with surprise and joy. She stepped back. Still holding my hands, she stated that no one had ever talked to her about turning her fears and worries over to God. That one thought had been such a witness to her. She hugged me again and thanked me for the prayer. We then finished cleaning up the dining room and kitchen.

The next morning, she met me in the kitchen as I was taking my luggage to the car. She had gotten up early and read an article about the Holy Spirit. She seemed excited. She had taught Sunday school, but this article had never made any sense to her. We agreed we had much to discuss when I returned. Much to my surprise, she asked me to pray for her to ask God to send the angels to watch over both of us. I knew her family would be there soon, but I also knew she was afraid to be alone in the house. I prayed that the angels would come and stay at the house. She hugged me again. She seemed like a different person to me.

She opened the old carriage gate, and I drove my car to the front of the driveway. As she closed the gate, I went inside the house through the front door to get Sugar Baby. When I returned to my car, Margaret, Daisy and Possum were standing behind the gate. I waved to Margaret and she waved back. The dogs' tails wagged their good-bye. I thought of this as a wonderful Christmas gift.

14

Christmastime in Knoxville was fun, but in the back of my mind was the thought, *What will it be like when I return to Abbeville?* Margaret and I talked once by phone during the two-week holiday. She had enjoyed her family during the Christmas holidays and had even traveled to Columbia to visit her son and his family.

When I returned to Abbeville one week after New Year's Day, the carriage gate was open, and Possum was sitting by the front door in her guard dog position. I stopped the car at the steps that went up to the porch. I could look straight across to see Possum. When she saw us, she followed the car as I continued through the open gate and then into the back carport. Margaret was gone, but Possum greeted us. The dog kept jumping and turning. I closed the gate. Sugar Baby and Possum were playing together. While I was taking the luggage inside, Margaret arrived and welcomed us back. We sat in the den by the fireplace and shared the events of our holidays. She said she had a wonderful sense of peace.

The following months brought a number of changes to my life. My mother had a stroke, which required me to travel back to Knoxville to see her. My brother Cannon, who lived there, moved into her house and assumed management of her care. I continued to teach counseling and Christian education at Erskine and worked at Troy and Lower Long Cane churches. Margaret seemed more relaxed, and Possum was calmer. I had purchased a house near Erskine College and planned to move to be closer to the school. One of my classmates needed a house at Due West (near the college), so I rented my house to him and his family. I continued renting at Margaret's house.

There was one situation when Possum got in trouble with the police. One Sunday morning, some bikers stopped in front of Bowie Hall. They rested their right legs on the three-foot high brick wall separating the sidewalk from the lawn. Possum did not like the commotion, so she nipped someone on the ankle. Margaret told the young policeman investigating the incident that Possum did not like the Sabbath being disturbed. When the policeman saw that one of the bikers had what looked like a beer can, he told her to keep the dog locked up for a week and ordered the bikers to meet him at the station before they left town. I did not realize that Possum had been converted and followed the Ten Commandments!

One warm day I needed to have a walk around the square. After a good brisk walk, I stopped at the Rough House to order some lunch for Margaret and me. Because of the poolroom in the back, the ladies had not been allowed inside the grill through the 1970s. This business was an Abbeville landmark, so I ordered some hot dogs and enjoyed the 1920s decor. Since Margaret informed me that she did not eat hot dogs, Possum and Daisy ate hers. I enjoyed the other two hot dogs with chili.

15

Later in the week, while I was preparing for my afternoon class, Margaret asked me one morning if I would drive up North Main Street to see the Smith-Perrin House. She wanted to see some furniture and did not want to go alone. I agreed. We drove to a house with four large columns. I noticed that we went to a side door. As we stood waiting for someone to come to the door, I also noticed that the steps to the front porch were gone. Several large magnolia trees shaded the porch, and the bottom tree branches covered the lawn. I had an uneasy feeling.

The door opened slowly. Mrs. Smith's daughter welcomed us. After Margaret introduced me, we followed the young lady through a dark corridor that came out in a backstairs hall. Dust was flying through the air. Light filtered in the hall from a window at the top of the stairs. After a moment of focusing, I was impressed by a large ornate staircase to the second floor. We walked into a front hallway. The large parlor door was locked. The young lady left us standing in a boxlike entrance room that had very fine and detailed woodwork. I felt as if we had broken into an ancient tomb.

Before us stood a large entrance door in the front hall that had sidelights with closed wooden shutters. The hall was dark, but I noticed a small room on the left of the entrance hall. I could see the daybed where someone napped in the past. The double doors were partly open. The old velvet drapes covered the windows of what I guessed was the music room at one time.

Margaret finally spoke and mentioned that the Smith family had in their possession the sofa and chairs that Jefferson Davis had sat on when he visited Abbeville. Suddenly, I realized the importance of the visit. She had tried to see the parlor set when she was a young married woman, but Mr. Smith Sr. had locked the antique furniture away.

Our hostess returned and apologized for taking so long. She was holding a large key. She put the key in the lock and turned it. She and I pushed on the right double door until it opened. It was hard to see at first, but there was one shutter partly open at the top of a window. It admitted enough light for us to see the parlor set: a sofa, two chairs covered in a dark green fabric, tables, and smaller chairs in the center of the room. The walls were filled with portraits of Abbeville citizens long gone. Very fine dust particles floated through the air. The ceilings were so high that I did think there might be a bat or two flying. In a short while, our hostess opened one of the inside window shutters. It was then that I could see Margaret smile.

I stepped back into the hall as she and our hostess negotiated about the furniture being on loan to the Burt-Stark Mansion. I could hear Margaret offer her warehouse on Trinity Street to store other family items. While they were talking, I stepped into the back hall to see the stairway again. The woodwork was outstanding, and the architecture made me think I was at Tara or Twelve Oaks Plantation in *Gone with the Wind*. As I explored the backstairs hall, I was impressed by the scale and beauty of each step and the wonderful hand railing.

I became aware of a dark cabinet behind the circular part of the stairs. When I opened the cabinet door, I realized I was looking at an expensive set of nineteenth-century French china. In fact, it was a double set of Old Paris china. My late wife had collected the plain white-and-gold pattern, but this was a green, gold, and painted flower set. I later learned it was the wedding china of Mr. and Mrs. Thomas Perrin from the 1850s. Most importantly, First Lady Mrs. Varina Davis had dined on this elegant service.

I walked to the front parlor and asked Margaret if I could speak with her. She seemed a little irritated at first until I opened the cabinet. She looked in, in shock. Margaret instantly recognized this set of Old Paris dishes but stated that she thought that they had long ago departed from Abbeville. She said that Mr. Perrin had used these dishes the night he entertained the war cabinet of Mr. Davis. She then turned and walked back into the large parlor. I could hear her asking to keep the china at the mansion. The young lady agreed, as long as it would not be removed from its cabinet. Her father had made the corner cabinet and wanted them to stay together.

They continued to talk about plans for the belongings of our hostess. I continued exploring the house and enjoyed the visual feast of beautiful classical Southern architecture. After some effort, I opened a shutter on the side of the front door. I could see how completely the magnolia trees shaded the house.

After the visit, we drove back to Bowie Hall. Margaret was so excited about the furniture. I had never seen her so elated. She even said that this gift to the Mansion was like God's grace; that is, you don't deserve it, but it shows up out of the blue. She turned to me and said that she had studied the book of Romans and now understood spiritual things.

I offered to get us some lunch, and she started phoning the board members. The board had a special afternoon tea and sherry party to welcome the furniture and china to the Mansion. Margaret said that the ladies were very appreciative of the gifts and sent a nice card. She thanked me for finding the china.

16

The Smith-Perrin House went up for sale and people "from off" (not Abbeville County) looked at the place. Finally, the house was cleaned out and sold. A new family came to town. They were Southern, so all the ladies approved of them. The ladies made their calls after a proper time of waiting for the family to get settled. Eventually, all the ladies liked the family.

The approval turned to shock and then Southern detachment when the new owners cut down the ancient magnolia trees in front of the house. The cutting was taken as an act against nature and tradition. Miss Sara and Miss Sallie reminded everyone that the trees had guarded the house for 150 years. One commented, "Trees are a gift from the garden of Eden." The consensus was that they were glad Mrs. Smith had not lived to see this tragic event, but they knew she would have forgiven the new people. Her response would have been most honorable, for she was a proper Christian Presbyterian lady from one of Abbeville's finest old families.

I began to hear the hurt and emotional attachment they had for the magnolia trees, especially as I listened to the ladies of the group. A new resolve was born to protect the trees of Abbeville. I wrote down the following notes from the comments they made about the magnolia trees:

A magnolia tree was usually planted in front of the house to protect the porch and windows in the event of a severe storm. The leaves are strong and flexible and dense so that rain and hail are repelled by the thick covering of the large green foliage.

As the tree grows taller, it produces a green-leafed lace curtain that shades the house from the heat of the morning or afternoon sun. It is as if the branches are layered one on top of the other with just the right amount of space between each layer. The openings between the leafy branches allow the breezes to glide through into the windows of the house.

The combination of protection, ventilation, and beauty gave birth to the love and admiration of the magnolia tree by the ladies of Abbeville. The glory of the magnolia buds and the white blossoms filled any house or garden with beauty and fragrance. Regularly, the tree gave a great summer surprise as the buds sprang open in the morning rain or at day's edge. Often, several pure white blooms came into view just outside of the dining room windows. Miss Ella told me that the array of such perfect creation gave breakfast an added enjoyment. The aroma of fried bacon and eggs, banana bread, grits, biscuits, and sausage gravy blended with the view of this beautiful flower gave the morning the perfect beginning needed for a steamy summer day.

I realized that the Burt-Stark ladies may have started out using the phrase "kiss the magnolia tree" as a way to joke with Miss Ella Perrin, but later the phrase became their secret code to signify their love for the mansion, Abbeville, and each other. This phrase took on the magnitude of loyalty to their private world. Only once did I hear Margaret use the phrase in front of outsiders. That one time was at the Belmont Inn Sunday buffet lunch when she was trying to get Miss Ella to stop talking about the history of the Perrin family. Margaret even lowered her voice as if some sacred incantation was being uttered. In response, Miss Ella smiled her nervous smile, looked straight at Margaret, and suggested that it was time for the guests to go back for dessert. The polished precision of Ella's response had the perfect rhythm that only an authentic lady could produce. The beauty of her unshakable control under pressure reminded me of a magnolia blossom gliding in the wind, untouched in a turbulent afternoon storm.

17

I started traveling to the Mayesville church on the weekends. One afternoon, Margaret firmly reminded me that she did not like to be in the house alone at night. This comment made me anxious until I heard her request. She asked me if I would pray that the angels would come and protect the house. All she wanted was for the two of us to meet before I left to have a prayer for the angels to surround the house. She reminded me that she had tried having women students stay in the summers while I was gone, and that young women did not understand her and could not get along with her. I decided to avoid speaking to that issue but quickly agreed that we would pray each time I left. She seemed satisfied with my answer and hurried off to some meeting. Several days later while walking down Trinity Street, I decided to have a special prayer time at Trinity Church. The door to the church building was open, so I went in.

The beautiful window with Christ as the Good Shepherd had been shipped there during the 1861–65 Yankee blockade of Charleston Harbor. I thought that miraculous event must have taken many angels, so I spent some time praying for a protective angel to come to Bowie Hall. "(Angels) are ministering spirits sent forth to minister to the heirs of salvation" (Hebrews 1:14). I had learned from my grandmother to claim the promises and wait for God to answer. If God could direct His angels to transport a large, fragile stained-glass window through the Yankee-controlled Charleston Harbor, He could send an angel to Abbeville's Greenville Street. I relaxed and went on my way.

Trinity Episcopal Church

Spring came, and Margaret began to work on presenting the city of Abbeville with her "barn" on Trinity Street. I picked up some lunch for us one day. She told the story of meeting one city official who did not like her. She explained how nice she had been to him as he bragged on his new silk suit and the money that purchased it. She asked me bluntly if I thought the person had any "background." I said I was not sure. She reiterated how nice she had been to him and that refined Southerners do not brag on their expensive possessions. "People of quality know what to say!" She left that topic quickly by saying that she loved the town of Abbeville and wanted to give her barn as a gift to the town so that there would be a passageway from the square to the parking lots behind Trinity Street. It would make an ideal event setting for wedding receptions or Saturday markets. She paused a moment, stating that Abbeville had come a long way in restoration.

She then said, "You know, I decided in college I would marry an Abbeville man. Mr. Willie Bowie was so handsome in his Citadel uniform. I had three different men I could have married, but I chose Willie Bowie. We were so in love. I got him *and* Abbeville. It worked out so well. Back then, we went to great parties. We danced almost all night at the Francis Marion ballroom in Charleston. My mother let me go to the Citadel party in Charleston only because my aunt went as my chaperone. I had a small silver purse with a fan attached. There was no air conditioning then." She paused, and we both sat in silence.

"It took Willie a long time to go. He was ill, and I tried to take care of him. Every day of our life together, I picked out his clothes. We had a great life. His sister, Janie Vance, was the hardest loss. She died earlier in my life. She had cancer. I would go to Chester and stay with her all day. I had a cook back in those days. Janie Vance asked me what I know about dying. She thought I knew everything. I acted so confident. I would take her hand, pat it and say, 'Everything will be fine.' As she grew sicker, she continued to ask me, 'What do you know about dying?'" Margaret paused and looked away. "I wish I had known about the Holy Spirit's resurrection work. Church back then was about being a good, moral person." Tears rounded down her face as we sat in silence. She dabbed her cheeks with a handkerchief. She paused and went on to say, "Janie Vance thought I knew everything. We were like sisters. I loved her so much. I should have said something about heaven that would have given her some comfort. I stayed with her until the end. Her husband, Robert Betts, was so loyal to her. In the end, her pastor came. He must have known because he prayed about angels. I have to forgive myself, but I wish I had known. She was so beautiful and generous."

The lunch we were eating had grown cold. She stood up. I said I was sorry for her losses. Margaret replied that I had also been there with my wife. We agreed that loss is so hard. The recounting of her losses was difficult to hear. It hurt. That day I realized I had come a long way since when my wife died on December 1, 1990. In some mysterious way, healing had taken place. The loss did not hurt as much as in the years before.

18

During the school year, I usually taught a class in Charleston at one of Erskine's teaching sites. Each summer, I would return to the town for a reunion lunch with some of the students and have a meeting with the site coordinator. I liked to see the students, socialize, and gather feedback on the teaching and application of my course. Margaret's minister, Reverend Phil Clarke, and his wife Ann had moved to Charleston in their retirement. She often talked about how she missed them. She knew I went to Charleston each summer. She found an antique show she and the Clarkes wanted to attend. She asked if I she could go with me to the "Holy City" of Charleston. Margaret stayed with the Clarkes on the Isle of Palms, and I stayed in Mount Pleasant.

On Sunday, the Clarkes went to church, and Margaret was so late getting ready that we missed the service. We drove downtown, toured the Battery, and drove up Meeting Street to the Mills House Hotel to wait for the Clarkes for Sunday lunch. The Mills House was remodeled in the early 1970s. The hotel had hosted Robert E. Lee when he toured the fortification at Charleston in 1861. The story was that he had to leave the hotel because the Great Charleston Fire was so intense. Of course, Margaret repeated this history to me until I let her out at the front door. The doorman, Clarence Davis, opened the car door and helped her up the steps. I could hear her thanking and charming him as she went into the hotel. I parked the car and met her in the lobby.

The hotel dining room had a high ceiling. Marble steps led down to a beautiful hall where we waited to be seated. Two dining rooms contained tables with white tablecloths and Chippendale chairs. The arched Palladian glass doors allowed light to flood the rooms. The fountain and flowers in the courtyard were colorful and manicured. The hostess seated us in the second dining room. Our table was near two large arched windows with closed West Indian shutters. A potted palm stood behind the table. The light in the room was softened as it came through the large shutters. We viewed the menu and talked about Charleston.

At one point in the conversation she said she had something to tell me before the Clarkes arrived. She had my complete attention. I put the menu down and turned to look directly at her. I noticed a smile on her face. She said that one night last winter, while I was away teaching, she had had trouble with her heart, which started going out of rhythm. She realized that her heart was acting up, so she got down out of her bed and started to reach for her bedside phone. She stated that she was quite afraid at that point. Then she realized or sensed that someone was standing at the foot of the two beds in her room. A powerful and calming presence was with her. She realized that her heart had gone back into rhythm. She was silent for a second but continued smiling. Before I could say anything, she added, "It was the angel we have prayed for. The angel was right in the room, and I am not afraid now!"

I was so surprised and overcome with joy that all I could say was, "How wonderful, how wonderful!" I was surprised that she related such a personal instance in her life, but we had prayed often for an angel's presence. My grandmother said, "Claim the promises and wait." We had done just that. I could see her happiness. She was freed from her fears. We celebrated. I think I ate two desserts that day.

My sense of awe and wonder was mixed with a slight sense of disorientation. My late wife and I sat at this same table in 1985. My mind was flooded with memories of August 18, 1985, when I had encountered an angel at St. Philip's Church in Charleston. That

Sunday, as Laura and I stood for the first hymn, I experienced the presence of a large white-winged angel standing behind us. The congregation was singing, "Surely God is my salvation. I shall trust and not be afraid" (Isaiah 12:1–6). I stood in the pew and could not stop crying as my wife kept looking over at me. Finally, I was able to stop my tears. When we got to the Mills House dining room, I told Laura about the wonderful and powerful healing appearance.

I was amazed that Margaret now was telling me about the appearance on Greenville Street. She and I were sitting at the same table in the same hotel dining room in the same city, Charleston. God must have a wonderful sense of humor in His ordering of events. I felt empowered in 1985, and I felt empowered and thankful as Margaret related her miracle to me. A promise had become a reality. Now we were blessed with an angel at Bowie Hall.

When Margaret visited Knoxville in the summer after her conversion, she stayed with Judy and David Birdwell. At a dinner party given in her honor by my friend Joy Matthews, Margaret related that since she received the Holy Spirit, "her eyes had been opened." She said that she had taught the book of Romans years before, but only now did she understand it.

19

Life seemed to fall into a pattern at Bowie Hall. I taught at Erskine and preached at various churches and continued visiting the sick and shut-ins. Margaret worked in tourism for the town and the Burt-Stark Mansion. She enjoyed her family and used the lake house more for their gatherings. When her granddaughter Amelia got married, Margaret was pleased. She bragged about her grandchildren but told others, "In Abbeville, we do not want to hear about your illnesses or your grandchildren. Keep it to yourself." Often she added, "Please."

Her family gave her a surprise ninetieth birthday party at the Belmont Inn in August. The entire dining room was filled with family and friends. Her son Flynn had a large cake made that was shaped like the Burt-Stark Mansion. The cake was beautiful and only part of it was eaten. The tables filled the dining room and the lobby. She was surprised and pleased. She wanted pictures with her grandchildren and family. The governor sent her a message of congratulations.

After everyone left for the party, I locked in Possum and Daisy, Possum's puppy, on the back porch. (My dog, Sugar Baby, had died the Christmas before.) We thought that the enclosed porch would keep Possum at home. I then closed the old carriage gate. During the party, a waitress I knew informed me that Possum was on the front verandah. She knew Miss Margaret and Possum and asked me what she should do. I went out on the front verandah. Possum was looking up at me, wagging her brush-like tail. I bent down, patted her head, and talked to her. She had come for the party. I got her some water and a small piece of cake.

In time, Margaret came out on the verandah and petted Possum. The image of a small, gray-headed lady in a black silk dress and pearl necklace with large diamond earrings, patting a dog on the verandah, gave everyone a good laugh. Later, Miss Ella and all of Margaret's friends sat around Margaret as she opened her gifts and cards. It was wonderful to see all the people who loved her. She stated that she was not used to getting all this attention. Margaret was totally surprised by the party that her son Flynn had worked so hard on. Her eyes danced as she saw the cake and all the people. She went around and thanked everyone for coming. It was a fine evening. She enjoyed having her younger friends, Cynthia Jeffries and Jeane Nichols, her favorite niece, there.

As the party came to an end, I got Possum to walk with me back to Bowie Hall. Our journey was a slow, hot walk, but I got her home. The heat began to lessen as Possum and I sat on the front porch of Bowie Hall. The sky had turned red with white layers in between. I had a glass of iced tea and gave Possum two cookies. I reflected on the events of the day's celebration as we waited for everyone to return. The people had looked elegant. Senator Billy O'Dell and his attractive wife were present as well as other officials. Misses Sallie, Ella, Sara, and Ruthie Harris were adorned in their family pearls and diamonds. One lady told us her diamond necklace had not been out of the bank vault since 1975. I was not sure what to say except that her necklace was lovely.

There are times when you think that day would make a perfect ending to one's story. As Possum and I sat there in the late summer afternoon, that thought came to my mind. This day was a "harmony day" when everything was loving, peaceful, and in harmony. The people were handsome and supportive, and the town was historic and beautiful. I thought of a Margaret quote, "Abbeville has come a long way from May 1865 when there was hardly any food even to feed President Davis."

That night, all the lights were on at Bowie Hall as we continued to visit and celebrate. Flynn brought the cake back to Bowie Hall.

Some people gave cards with donations for the Burt-Stark Mansion in honor of Margaret. She enjoyed her family and friends that night. Even her son Bill, who was not well, enjoyed it. Possum settled down and guarded the front door. Margaret would not let me give her a second piece of cake. She told me I had to remember that Possum was part wild dog and sweets were not good for her.

Margaret Bowie and Doug White

20

Margaret continued to work hard for tourism in Abbeville. Joan Davis came often. They planned and promoted the town. She often consulted with Janie Wiltshire about promoting the Mansion. She went to many meetings and dinners. She was invited to some kind of reunion dinner and lecture on the War for Southern Independence. She said she was quite surprised when someone asked her what she thought of the war. She replied that no one loved the South more than she did, but the war was a total waste of men, animals, and resources. She said that an entire generation of men was destroyed. "My husband's aunts never married because their beaux were killed in the war." In her childhood, one could see the destruction of the "Yankee Invasion." Margaret smiled and added that she imparted her comments in a proper ladylike manner in order to avoid any controversy.

The fall passed quickly that year. The police showed up once to ask where Possum was. Margaret said she assumed the dog was in the basement. The police drove off after walking around the back driveway. Possum showed up later that night for her dinner. Margaret thought that Abbeville, South Carolina, had the best police force in the South, as fine as the Due West police, who made that little village the safest in South Carolina.

Margaret had known Mr. Glenn Teachey for some time when he and his wife Betty moved to a historic house on North Main

Street. Each year, they had a black-tie Christmas party. I drove Misses Margaret, Sallie and Ada to the event. The charm of the ladies was in full force that night. Mr. and Mrs. Teachey greeted us at the door. The grand front hallway was decorated with beautiful Christmas ornaments, and a large chandelier lighted the hall. Glenn always hugged the ladies. I noticed how giddy they acted. Mrs. Teachey was an attractive woman. She welcomed us and offered us food and drinks. The ladies went into the dining room, and I stepped into the large front parlor to speak to a vice president from the college. After a while, Miss Sallie brought me a cup of Gypsy with just the right amount of flavoring. She went back to the ladies, while I stopped to speak to Lucia and Thurmond Bishop, who looked quite elegant. Another man stepped to the side of our conversation and gave me a small envelope. He walked away. Before putting it in my pocket, I noticed the envelope was addressed to Mrs. Margaret Bowie. That puzzled me. About that time, Mr. Teachey asked everyone to step into the parlor where several toasts were offered. This gentleman in black tie reminded me of a Southern John Wayne with elegance. I knew Margaret had worked hard to get him to move to Abbeville.

We visited, ate, and toasted. We left the party happy to celebrate another Abbeville Christmas. We got in the car and viewed the lights on North Main Street. We drove toward the square. Miss Sallie talked about the party and wonderful restoration the Teacheys had done on their home. Miss Ada commented that there should be magnolia trees in the park coming up to the house. Miss Sallie agreed. Margaret listened to their comments and then told them they could kiss the magnolia trees on Miss Ella's lawn if they liked. Everyone laughed and celebrated that we lived in the old town.

As we passed the Burt-Stark Mansion, Margaret reminded everyone about her upcoming Christmas party. Ella thoughtfully pointed out the First Baptist Church on the opposite side of the street. The beautiful four-columned building was decorated with large elegant Christmas wreaths. On the same side of the street, the ornate First Presbyterian Church had an impressive combination of lights and greenery. The two churches on the other side of North Main Street were equally beautiful in their Christmas attire. We turned onto the square to view the dazzling lights and colorful decorations. The tall Christmas tree at the south end of the square had large round ornaments with both white and colored lights. The town looked so festive.

I took the other ladies to their homes. We arrived back at Bowie Hall. While we were in the den, I gave Margaret the note and told her about the man. She opened the envelope and read the note out loud. It stated that she needed to get Possum out of town. Someone was going to pick her up. There was no signature or explanation. She gave me the note and sat down on the sofa. She said that she could not understand some people being so misguided. Possum did rove all over town, but other dogs did the same. She had never bitten any innocent person.

As she was forming a plan, I turned on the gas logs. We sat by the fireplace. After a time of concentration, she announced that she would take Possum to the lake to stay with Bill, her son. Bill loved dogs. It was the perfect solution. Possum was packed into Margaret's white Cadillac the next morning.

She spent a month at the lake. The only complication was to tell Gene Smith without alarming him. (He was the elderly man who cooked Possum a complete breakfast of two eggs, toast and grits every morning.) He lived on Chestnut Street. After being told, he promised to keep our secret. I finally understood why Possum climbed the six-foot-high fence each morning and disappeared before anyone was awake.

Bill brought Possum home in late January. He said she was a good guest and a great traveler. I noticed that Bill was thinner.

21

That winter, Margaret entertained a Southern history expert who came to investigate the Burt-Stark Mansion, especially the items loaned by Mrs. Smith's daughter. The board had a luncheon at the Grill and a catered dinner at Bowie Hall. I was traveling then, but I heard the Burt-Stark ladies were all charmed by the man and even more by the details of his research. Much to their surprise, he liked the early 1900s bathroom at the Mansion. He thought it was a "real jewel." The antique china was validated as the Perrin wedding china, and the sofa and chairs covered with the 1850–1860s dark green horsehair upholstery were those Mr. Davis and his cabinet would have sat on. The carpet fragment was in the house in 1860 and most likely in the men's parlor.

Miss Ella said he was so impressed by the Mansion that he asked them if they had the Confederate seal there. She said she related the story that Judah Benjamin, the Secretary of State of the Confederacy, had asked her ancestor, Mr. Perrin, for a hammer to crush the seal so it would not fall into the hands of the approaching Yankees. She said that Mr. Perrin did not want the seal destroyed in his home, so he told him to throw it in the Savannah River when he crossed the next morning. Margaret interrupted Miss Ella and told her that the expert was joking about their having the seal.

Miss Ella seemed determined that he was not joking and continued telling her story. She stated that Mr. Benjamin stayed with Mr. Perrin, Miss Ella's ancestor, while the president stayed across the street. When Mr. Benjamin was ready to leave the next morning, he asked Mr. Perrin to mail him his trunk. He explained that he hoped to escape to England, and he would write and give him his address. Mr. Perrin agreed to keep the trunk and indeed sent it to Mr. Benjamin in England. Mr. Perrin said that the trunk was very heavy. He thought the seal and some of the gold were in it. Miss Ella said she thought the expert needed to know what Mr. Perrin thought happened to the seal. We all agreed Ella's saga was an interesting story.

Spring seemed to come early that year. One morning, I was fixing my breakfast cereal when the phone in the kitchen rang. When I answered it, a man's voice asked to speak to Margaret and then requested that I stay with her while she received the message. I stepped into the back hall and told her she had a phone call. After a short time, she took the call. As she listened, she turned away from me, facing the kitchen window over the sink. All she said was "Thank you for the call" and "Go ahead." When she slowly turned to walk toward me, she was pale, and her eyes were full of tears. She then stated very slowly that Gene Smith, who cooked Possum's breakfast every morning, found her dead near his back steps. She had apparently died early that morning. He wanted to bury her in his back garden, to which she agreed. "We can go down later," she said. "You know, I found her right before Christmas. She had four puppies on Christmas morning." She stopped talking and turned to look out the window. Then there was silence.

I was standing by the center counter of the kitchen. I picked up a white paper towel, put down my cereal bowl, and stepped toward the sink. She said that she knew Possum was growing old but did not expect her death now. "She was the sweetest dog! Why did people think she was a biter? She never bit any innocent person." She repeated that Possum was the sweetest dog. As I handed her the paper towel to wipe her tears, she turned slightly and asked me, "Well, will Possum be in heaven?"

I was in shock about Possum. One thought came to my mind, and out it came. "The Bible says that the wolf will lie down with the lamb in the new heaven and new earth."

Almost before I could finish speaking, she said, "Tell me no more. That is wonderful!" As she turned and looked out the window, I handed her another paper towel. She took it in her left hand and dabbed her cheek. She extended her right hand, and I took her hand in my left hand.

We stood looking at the six-foot-high stone wall that Possum had so often climbed. We cried together. There was silence again. Then she repeated that Possum was the sweetest dog and never bit anyone. She then dropped my hand and said that she had to go. "You never leave unless you say good-bye to a dog," she stated and rushed off to get dressed.

I had to get to class, but we were still in shock! The grief fluctuated from shock to denial, to hurt, and then to disorientation. We kept talking about Possum. The pain would come and then lift.

Spring arrived with a somber mood as it became apparent that Margaret's oldest son Bill was quite ill. That summer, she focused on his care. Possum's death seemed to be a preparation for the loss of Bill. He died in September of 2004. Her other son, Flynn and her family gathered around her and were supportive. She talked to me about how disoriented and alone she felt. We talked about how grief makes all of us feel detached.

22

One day, as I was coming in from school, Margaret asked me to come into the front living room. She told me she was thinking of going to live in Columbia at Still Hopes Episcopal Retirement Community. There was a moment of silence. Then she said she was almost ninety-five years old. She wondered if the angel at Bowie Hall would go with her. She smiled, and I smiled. I assured her that we would pray, and the angel would be with her. She thanked me for praying and then she said that she had great comfort that she would see her son again.

She said that when I had read 2 Thessalonians 4:13–18 at his funeral, she knew it was true that his spirit was now with Christ, and there would be a day when Christ would come back and we would all meet the Lord in the air. She paused and smiled before saying, "You know, there will be a new heaven and a new earth, and the wolf and the lamb will be together." She continued by saying that she hoped that Possum would be one of the many dogs in the new earth.

I smiled and told her that I hoped so too. The thought came to my mind that this was not the time to get too deep. I affirmed that we were to comfort each other that we would all be together with the Lord. We hugged and talked about moving to Columbia. We agreed it was a good idea to be closer to her remaining son and the grandchildren. I knew she was ambivalent about moving. She stated that she had some strong board members at the Burt-Stark Mansion. Hal and Barbara Freese and Sally and Billy Hughes were members now, so she could step down and let them run the mansion. She ended the conversation by saying that she did not really like the small house

I had purchased in Due West. I assured her that I would not move until after she had gone to Columbia. I wondered if she would really make the move.

One afternoon, she stated that she had decided to go to the debutante ball at the armory. She had a talk with Marilyn and Buddy Reid. She was excited to be going with them to the debutante ball. They had been friends for years. She and other ladies had reorganized the presentation ball after World War II. She said she had been presented in the 1920s, and there was too much drinking back then. "You know, this will be my last debutante ball. I have always enjoyed them. I have loved the old town. Marilyn and I have worked on all kinds of promotions. She and Buddy are quality people."

Margaret Bowie

I told her I was glad she was going and wanted to see her before she left. She looked outstanding that night. Marilyn came in the house to help Margaret to the car. She agreed to take a picture of Margaret at the event for me. When she returned, we sat in the front parlor by the fireplace as she talked about the various young ladies who were presented and her mixed feelings about leaving Abbeville. She stopped talking for a time. Then she said that she had to talk to Ella about her move to Columbia. Ella was like her child, and she had guided and cared for Ella much of Ella's adult life. She reminded me that Ella was the same age as Bill, her deceased son. I agreed with her that telling her was going to be hard. She asked me to pray, and we did.

Several weeks later, she called a meeting of her closest friends at the Burt-Stark Mansion. She told Misses Sara, Sallie, and Ella about her plans to go to Columbia. I decided to walk our new dog, Gracie, down to the mansion to see if I could help Miss Ella. I knew Margaret and Ella were still hurting from Bill's death. As I walked Gracie around the front carriage park, I noticed that Misses Sara and Sallie came out of the house and drove away. Finally, Margaret and Ella exited and stood on the front porch. Ella had a white napkin or handkerchief in her hand as if she had been crying. Once in a while, they would point toward the church spires and the street coming up to the house as if discussing some event that happened there. In time, I saw Margaret take Ella's hand, and then Ella hugged Margaret.

Later, Margaret told me that Ella could not believe that she could leave Abbeville. She needed Margaret to stay. Margaret related to her that they had been strong women, but it was time to fall back on the angels. "Sometimes letting go is the thing to do," she said. They stood in silence. After a time, Ella confessed, "Margaret, once I did kiss the magnolia tree, and it was not that bad." Miss Margaret said, "Oh, Ella! You are such a child. I love you! Let's go down to the Grill and have dinner, child. I don't know what you are going to do without me!" They stood there on the porch in the warm spring sunshine as they hugged each other.

The move to the Still Hopes residence in Columbia was hastened when Margaret had a slight stroke. Fortunately, she had no aftereffects. She had a great apartment with much of her best furniture. Her son Flynn and family were supportive. Her old friend Cass Pressly called her every night, and her niece, Jeane Nichols, visited her twice a month.

23

Several weeks after Margaret's departure, I called Miss Ella to see how she was doing. She related that they were carrying on their duties at the Mansion. She was exploring the possibility of going to live at the Due West Retirement Center. We agreed that was a good choice. She said resting on the angels was difficult at times, but she thought she was doing well.

I was a little surprised when several weeks later, I got a call from Miss Ella on a Friday. She asked if I could meet with her at the Belmont Inn in the "Margaret Parlor," as she called the room in the left back corner. We met there Saturday morning at eleven o'clock. When I arrived, she said she did not want lunch but needed to talk. Her habitual nervous smiling was gone, replaced by a serious tone. She seemed anxious. We sat on the large Victorian sofa. When I asked her what happened, she came right out with her question, "Is Possum really dead?"

I was surprised. I assumed we were going to talk about retirement homes. I asked her what had happened to make her ask that question. She explained that she had been called several times to the Burt-Stark Mansion by the Abbeville police who were answering the mansion's alarm calls. She stated that it reminded her of the days when Possum would hide in the mansion and Margaret would have to go down with the police to let her out. Ella said that when she and the policeman got to the mansion, the alarm was ringing even though there was no one—man *or* dog—there. Quite puzzled, I proposed that maybe it was insects or dust that set off the alarm. Miss Ella said, "It is so strange because it's about the same time that

Possum would set off the mansion alarm." She wondered if the dog really was dead. I tried to think about what else to say. Suddenly, it came to mind to tell her to go see Mr. Gene Smith, who had buried Possum in his back garden. After a moment of silence, she turned quietly to face me. She said, "I will do just that. Gene is a longtime friend of mine."

Miss Ella seemed calmer, and she changed the subject at that point. She related how much she missed Margaret and that Abbeville was not the same without her friend. We agreed. She then brought up her lung condition. She said that "Mr. Puff" was going to get her. She should never have been involved with him. I asked her if she was talking about her smoking. She changed the subject, saying "I am going to call Gene Smith. The policemen think I am mentally off when I tell them that the alarm was set off by a dead dog." I told her I did not think she needed to tell them that thought. She got up. We walked through the lobby and out on the verandah. I told her that we needed to add her name to the parlor, the Ella and Margaret parlor. She smiled. She reached for my arm. I steadied her. She seemed fragile.

As we slowly walked down the steps of the Belmont Inn, the town square came into view. A spring breeze cooled us but also carried the full fragrance of all the spring flowers. Dogwoods, azaleas, and other flowers gave Abbeville a refreshing and invigorating beauty. I walked her to her car, and she drove off.

I walked around the square and got two hot dogs at the Rough House. I sat on a bench in the square and ate, dreaming of covered wagons filled with Confederate gold circling the square. I dreamed of walking around the square with my late wife Laura and Margaret picking Possum up on the square so many Christmases ago. All that was in the past. All those events came flooding into my mind. The day was a beautiful spring event, a time to celebrate and give thanks for life—past and present.

24

I visited Margaret in Columbia. She loved to show me the chapel at Still Hopes and introduce me to people she met. She had a beautiful apartment. She always knew more about Abbeville than I did, thanks to her friend Cass and the *Press and Banner*. In the summertime, we would sit on the porch of the old Still Hopes Mansion. Often Flynn and Anne, her daughter-in-law would arrange for us to go out to dinner in Columbia. She would talk about events in her life. She said she regretted that she did not realize the importance of visiting those in hospitals and retirement centers. She said if she could do it over, she would change that. Once she related that the angel had come with her. Being over ninety years old was not easy. She often came to Abbeville for visits, and we would always go to the Grill. Her son and family were supportive of her visits. We discussed Abbeville history or some current event every time.

Several weeks before exams, I drove down to Columbia. Much to my surprise, she was in bed. We spoke briefly, and then I just sat by her bed as she slept. Before I left, I prayed and told her I loved her and I would see her soon. I knew it would be in the next world. I prayed silently. She was weak, but she awoke and reached out her hand for mine. I told her, "Margaret, I love you" and said good-bye. She answered, "Me too."

As I rose to leave, she kept holding my hand. I told her again that I loved her. After a time of silence, I started to leave but various scriptures came to my mind. I bent down and said to her, "There is a beautiful city out there called heaven." She kept holding my hand. Tears flowed down my face. I told her she did not have to be afraid because the Lord would come for her and take her across in the end. She tightened her grip on my hand. I repeated, "When the end comes, the Lord will send His angels out to take you across. Don't be afraid. The Lord has already opened the gates." I sat in silence, holding her hand until she fell completely asleep. I placed her hand on the bed and slowly stood up. She looked peaceful. I repeated to myself, "Blessed are those who die in the Lord." I slipped out of the room. I knew the end was coming.

I drove back to Due West to continue my work at Erskine. The end of the semester was full of long workdays and exams. I had dinner with Carole and Charles Dawson and asked them to pray. I also called Jack and Evelyn and several Knoxville friends to pray for Margaret. My denial about loss had worked for me for about three months after my wife died. I counted on the same mechanism to get me through exams and the funeral. I prayed that the deep pains of grief would be delayed.

Flynn, Margaret's son, called me midweek of the exams. He told me she was gone and asked if I would officiate at her funeral. I stated that I would be honored. We agreed we would discuss the details later. I told him I was sorry. He said his mother had lived a good long life in ninety-seven years. We hung up. I was numb.

That afternoon, I was grading exam papers. I continued doing so. One student had written a paper on the benefits of the cross with an emphasis on Christ's victory over death. The paper explored the implications for grief counseling with people. I started to become emotional. I let my dog Gracie run around in the yard. She knew I was hurting and kept coming back to the porch where I was sitting. I patted her and assured her that I was all right. I reminded myself that I was a trained counselor and professor. I had to use all my skills to get through the days ahead.

25

The funeral was on Saturday morning at the Harris Funeral Home. The day was one of those beautiful spring days with mild sun, a nice cool breeze, and the fragrance of flowers. Everyone was dressed in their finery. Before I put on my black robe for the service, I was standing by the front pews. I heard two ladies talking loudly about another lady, saying, "Look at her. Look how she is all made up." The other lady said, "Well, you know what we say in Abbeville, 'Powder and paint can make us what we ain't.'" I laughed to myself and thought, *What would Margaret say about gossiping in Abbeville?* I laughed inside, but at the same time, I thought about the power of the resurrection.

Janie Wiltshire gave the eulogy. She did an outstanding job. She reminded us how deeply Margaret loved Abbeville, listing all the service work she had done. Margaret had been honored by the state of South Carolina when she received the Palmetto Award in 1997.

My text scripture for the service was Hebrews 12:22–25. I pointed out that Margaret was now in heaven not by her works, but by the gift of the Holy Spirit that she had received when she was eighty-seven years old on Christmas Eve. I also stated that no matter what Margaret did or said to anyone in Abbeville while on Earth, she was now completed in heaven because of God's mercy. She was now one of those "spirits of just men made perfect" written about in verse 23. I concluded the service, saying, "Let us rejoice and hope that Margaret loves heaven as much as she loved Abbeville. Let us rejoice and give thanks." At the gravesite, I read 2 Thessalonians 4:16–18 and spoke about the second coming of Christ.

Flynn asked me to come back to the house and visit the family. I talked with Flynn and his wife and the children. Amelia, Margaret's granddaughter, thanked me for reminding them about the second coming. She remembered that part from when we buried her Uncle Bill, Margaret's oldest son. Amelia, Jim, and Flynn Jr. thanked me.

I stepped out on the back porch briefly and patted Daisy. She was going to a new home. It was hard to realize she was Possum's puppy because she had solid white fur. She jumped up and down. I patted her and tried to say good-bye. I could feel the wave of grief coming, but I tried to block the pain.

I picked up a sandwich and iced tea, put it on a dinner plate, and went into the large front parlor. I sat on the yellow silk Victorian chair and viewed the room where I had so often reviewed my sermons for Sunday services. I knew this would be the last time friends and family would fill the home.

I came to Abbeville as a widower who wanted to take a yearlong break from my counseling practice. My break turned into fourteen years. I lived in Bowie Hall for twelve of those years. It had been twelve wonderful years. At times, it was like a time warp. The perceptions of Margaret and Ella were often right out of the year 1860. Ella's cousin warned me about ghosts and shadows. I had seen many. Margaret was now safely in heaven. I gave thanks for the twelve years and wondered if the angel would come back to Bowie Hall or go on a new assignment.

My heart was breaking, but I thought of God's plan. The year right after my wife's death, I would read Psalm 138:8. God's purpose was promised in that verse. I claimed it and searched for it. My life was broken. It had been God's plan for me to come to Abbeville. I gave thanks as I ate my sandwich. It had been a wonderful adventure. I experienced God's healing and love. God's powerful healing love propelled us forward. My life had been blessed by the beautiful and steel-willed lady who was now in heaven. With the death of Margaret Bowie, we knew the end of an era had come. The wonderful village of Abbeville would go on, but it would never be the same. I learned to love Abbeville. She was a contagious teacher. She had shown others how to love the town. I thought of the secret code words, *kiss the magnolia tree*. I understood it now. Margaret had valued and served Abbeville, and she had given me that same affection. I had learned to "kiss the magnolia tree."

I took a last look at the spacious fireplace, the many Victorian chairs, the two antique sofas, and the large window with pale yellow silk draperies. The polished mahogany center table anchored the room. The large parlor had been a beautiful sanctuary for me. The Holy Spirit opened my mind repeatedly to new ideas in this space. Not only had Margaret received the illumination of the scripture, but my understanding had been deepened. A thought came to my mind that my assignment was complete. It was time to try to let go. I got up and strolled around the room. As I walked to the entrance, it occurred to me that I needed to check on Ella.

26

Ella moved to the Due West Retirement Center. I lived near there, so I visited her one afternoon. We talked about the usual things. At the end of the visit, she said that the last time she worked at the Burt-Stark Mansion, she thought she heard Possum jump down off one of the upstairs beds. She missed the old place, but her imagination must have been working on her that day. I changed the subject and thanked her for all the work she had done for tourism in Abbeville. She thanked me for the compliment. She said, "Margaret and I were quite a team." I agreed with her. I asked her if she ever really did kiss the magnolia tree in her yard. She looked at me with a big smile and said, "I'm not telling. We were a special group with our own secret code." We laughed, and she hugged me. A friend came by, and I excused myself.

In the months that followed Margaret's death, I would take one or two flowers to her grave. I would give thanks for her and ask God to bless her in the heavenly city. I would never stay long. I would repeat, "Blessed are those who die in the Lord." The visit would help my grief.

On Friday, February 8, I realized I needed to go to the bank on business. I drove over to Abbeville about four in the afternoon. As I drove toward the town, I passed Upper Long Cane Cemetery. Suddenly, my mind was flooded with memories of the many Friday nights at Margaret's house. She so often had humorous stories about afternoon tourists who visited the Burt-Stark Mansion. Jack, Evelyn, Margaret and I would often go to the Grill for dinner and then come back to sit around the fireplace in the parlor.

I had that bittersweet sadness that comes with loss. My mind jumped back to the Christmas Eve when we prayed together. I thought of the richness and warmth of her presence. All at once, I realized I was driving in front of her house. Leaves partly covered the driveway. I realized something was sitting in front of the entrance door. I slowed down. As I drove past the house, I looked up the concrete stairs leading to the front door. There was a brown-and-black dog with a long, pointed nose. The dog looked out at me. I felt surprise and shock. I drove on to the bank. I could not believe what I had seen. The dog looked so much like Possum that I drove back to the house. The dog was still there. I pulled up in the driveway until I was parked next to the porch. When I stepped out of the car, the dog got up and walked across the porch. It jumped up on the wall that ran around the terrace and looked back at me. The pointy-nosed dog then disappeared over the wall at the west end of the terrace. It walked just like Possum with her "wiggly" movements. My mind tried to understand what I had just seen. I did not believe in ghosts. Maybe Miss Ella was right that Possum was still alive, but she would be so old. Was it one of the puppies Margaret had rescued? I always assumed the puppies were white. Maybe it *was* a canine ghost!

I got back into my car and sat there thinking. Maybe I was seeing things, I wondered. Suddenly, the impulse came to drive out to Margaret's grave. That late afternoon was cold, windy, and overcast. Fortunately, I had a wool coat in the car. I arrived at the graveyard and walked out to the Bowie plot. The wind picked up, so I put the coat on as I walked. As I approached the grave, I could see that her monument had been set. The words and design were beautiful. The inscription noted her name, dates, and a record of her long service to Abbeville. Suddenly, I had a sense of peace that comes from sensing a loving, ordering presence in the world. My mind and feelings rested in the mysterious power of His purposes.

I stood there a long time, smiling. She had been a gift to Abbeville and to me. God's wonderful plan had given us the miracles of angels, healings, and redemption. All was well in the world. As I walked back to my car and drove back to Due West, I rejoiced.

The spring that followed that cold winter was one of beautiful flowers and robust greenery. While I still felt the loss at times, the pain had lessened. Ann Clarke called me one day and said she had returned from Charleston to Abbeville to check on their house on Chestnut Street. She related that as she came into town, she decided to drive through the square, up North Main, and onto Greenville Street. As she turned from Greenville onto Chestnut, there was a dog walking down the street that looked like Possum. I was not sure what to say, so I asked if she was sure. Ann reminded me that Possum had nipped at her years before. She stopped the car, but the dog was gone. We agreed to meet for dinner.

I arrived at the Grill first. When Ann arrived, we hugged. I helped her remove her colorful spring jacket. We were able to sit in Margaret's booth. Ann described the dog's appearance again. She talked about all the possibilities. I told her I could not explain it rationally. After a time of silence, Ann said, "You remember that Margaret had an angel appear to her, so anything can happen in Abbeville." I replied, "You are right. Sweet Possum could be roaming and protecting Abbeville as she always did. I hope she has not bitten anyone." We laughed and celebrated that we loved Margaret and Possum, and we, like Miss Ella, had kissed the magnolia tree.

To everything there is *a season, a time for every purpose under heaven: a time to be born, and a time to die; a time to plant, and a time to pluck* what is *planted; a time to kill, and a time to heal; a time to break down, and a time to build up; a time to weep, and a time to laugh; a time to mourn, and a time to dance.* (Ecclesiastes 3:1–4)

He has made everything beautiful in its time. Also, He has put eternity in their hearts, except that no one can find out the work that God does from beginning to end. I know that nothing is better for them than to rejoice, and to do good in their lives, and also that every man should eat and drink and enjoy the good of all his labor—it is the gift of God.
I know that whatever God does, it shall be forever. Nothing can be added to it, and nothing taken from it. God does it, *that men should fear before Him. That which is has already been, and what is to be has already been; and God requires an account of what is past.* (Ecclesiastes 3:11–15)

Though the Lord is on high, yet He regards the lowly; but the proud He knows from afar. Though I walk in the midst of trouble, You will revive me; You will stretch out Your hand against the wrath of my enemies, and Your right hand will save me. The Lord will perfect that which concerns me; Your mercy, O Lord, endures forever; do not forsake the work of Your hands. (Psalm 138:6–8)

Therefore, humble yourself under the mighty hand of God, that He may exalt you in due time, casting all your cares upon Him, for He cares for you. (1 Peter 5:6–7)

ABBEVILLE GYPSY

It would be unforgivable to publish the recipe for Abbeville
Gypsy, but if the reader will write the publisher, I will respond.

RECOGNITION

I would like to especially recognize the following women for their outstanding contributions to their communities:

My mother, Louise Rolen White
My aunts, Lillian M. White and Gladys E. Rolen
My mother-in-law, Mattie Bun Kissiah
My late wife, Laura Kissiah White
My wife, Nancy Dempster Kelly White
Lori Bertelkamp McKelvy
Ann McAfee Warwick
Kane Watson McAfee
Julia Taylor White

ACKNOWLEDGMENT

Grateful acknowledgment is made to the following for their support and efforts in the development of this book:

Nancy Bowman, typist and editor

Gail Corey, creative consultant and editor

Becky Harper, computer consultant and reader

Anne Dempster Taylor, reader

Lucia Bishop, artist of drawings of Possum and Abbeville

Patricia Hubbs, creative artist of the Abbeville map

Oscar Velasquez, artist, granted permission to use his drawing of the Belmont Inn

The Williamsburg Foundation, permission to use the print "Laurel Tree of Carolina" ca. 1743 by Mark Catesby from *The Natural History of Carolina, Florida, and the Bahamas*

Dave McMeekin, gave permission to use the print of the Burt-Stark Mansion from Wishcraft Workshop, owned by his late mother, Fran McMeekin

Karen Lewis, art reviewer

Sally W. Hughes, treasurer of the Burt-Stark Mansion

Susan Botts, owner of the Belmont Inn

Trez Clarke, granted permission to use portions of her late father's book, *A Visitor's Guide to Historic Abbeville, South Carolina*

Evelyn and Jack Cauley, supportive and wonderful friends

Cannon White, my brother who offered encouragement and support

Nancy White, helper with many aspects of the book

Special thank you to the team at Covenant Books

R. Douglas White

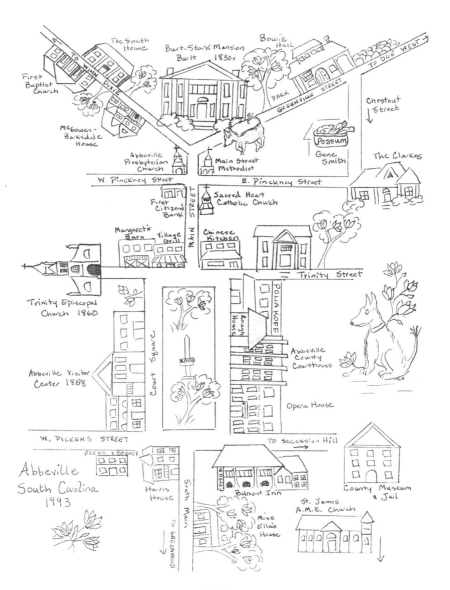

Map of Abbeville

A BRIEF HISTORY
OF ABBEVILLE

The Abbeville District came into being as a result of a treaty with the Cherokee Indians in 1755. It was in that year that British Royal Governor James Glenn conceived the idea of extending the borders of Charles Towne into the "backcountry," as the Charlestonians called the Piedmont section.

The governor arranged a meeting at "Saluda Old Town" with the Cherokee chiefs who were friendly toward the British. He persuaded the chiefs to agree to give up their claims to the larger part of upper South Carolina and move their tribes westward into the mountains of North Carolina and Tennessee.

When the threat of the Indians was removed, settlers from Pennsylvania, Virginia, North Carolina, and even Europe began an immigration movement into this area. The Scotch-Irish found that a well-defined wagon road, the Black Bear Trail, extended all the way from Pennsylvania to Georgia and furnished an easy approach to South Carolina.

The first record of settlement in the Abbeville area was on February 16, 1756, when Patrick Calhoun, his mother, sister, and three brothers arrived. They were accompanied by four other families. Some historians believe there were settlers in the general area as early as 1710. At any rate, the Calhouns, along with the four other families, settled at the intersection of two streams, one of which flowed into the Savannah River. The site was about seventeen miles south of Abbeville.

The region was almost an impenetrable forest with tall canes growing rampant in the fertile bottom land. These "cane breaks" also forced their way by brook and riverlet into the hills where the soil had depth. Patrick Calhoun, a surveyor or ranger, was so enthusiastic over this new land abounding with fish and game that he was largely responsible for founding the first settlement. Near the bold, clear stream, he built a home for his family. He called the creek "Long Cane." By 1758, there were perhaps forty families living in the settlement.

It was during this time that Andrew Pickens settled the present town at Abbeville. He chose the site of Abbeville because of the freshwater supply known as "the spring."

In 1760, the Cherokee broke their treaty with the new royal governor William Lyttleton and went on the warpath to recover their hunting grounds. A runner was sent from Fort Prince George to warn the settlers to escape to Augusta, but time had run out. On February 1, 1760, the Cherokee attack took place. The settlers were hopelessly outnumbered and fifty or more were killed by the Cherokees. Others were tortured, while some were taken captive.

After the Indians had retreated from their attack, the settlers gathered their remaining number and set out for Augusta. After a few years, most of them were back at Long Cane Settlement, ready to start anew. It was obvious that these hardy pioneers were strengthened by their adversities.

In 1764, some two hundred Huguenots fled the religious persecutions in France and settled in the Abbeville area. One of their number, Dr. John de la Howe, is given credit for naming Abbeville after his native town in France by that same name. The town of New Bordeaux was also named by him.

Andrew Pickens built a blockhouse near the Abbeville Village in 1767 for protection against the Indians. During the Revolutionary War, in which he served as a general, his blockhouse was named Fort Pickens.

Abbeville was organized as a unit of the state government in 1798. Starting in the 1820s, many fine homes and shops were built in Abbeville. Robert Mills, the famous architect, lived in Abbeville for a time and designed the third courthouse in 1829. The Burt-Stark mansion was built by Lawyer David Leslie in the 1830s. The town of Abbeville was incorporated as a municipality in 1840. In 1844, the Abbeville Press and Banner opened for business. The town became known as a center for upcountry social gatherings and political events.

Abbeville is known as the "birthplace" and the "deathbed" of the Confederacy. On November 22, 1860, a mass meeting was held on Secession Hill at which time it was unanimously voted to adopt the Ordinance of Secession. The ordinance was adopted the following month at the State Convention in Charleston, and South Carolina became the first state to secede from the Union.

On May 2, 1865, President Jefferson Davis met with his cabinet and war council for the last time at the home of his friend, Major Armistead Burt. A week later, President Davis was captured in Irwinville, Georgia, and served two years in prison at Fortress Monroe, Virginia. Varina Davis, his wife, had stayed for two weeks before Mr. Davis arrived at the Burt home.

Abbeville did not suffer physical effects as a result of the war, but it did suffer from disastrous fires in the 1870s. The Square was redeveloped and rebuilt, giving it a similar appearance to the way it looks today.

From 1880 to 1890, there was great activity in construction of homes and churches. After the turn of the century, the Eureka Hotel was built in 1903, and across the street, in 1908, the Opera House/Courthouse complex was built. It was during these times that Abbeville prospered. It was only when the boll weevil killed off King Cotton that Abbeville fell on hard times.

Comeback was a slow process, but in the late 1960s, historic restorations began taking place. Approximately three hundred properties are now listed in the National Register of Historic Places. As a result of historic restorations and revitalization of the town, Abbeville has moved to the forefront in business, culture, and commerce. Industry and tourism have developed to the point that Abbeville is now one of the prime locations in the entire state. With continued efforts on the part of all concerned, Abbeville will continue to become a better place today for a better place tomorrow.

This information is adapted from a book printed in 1990, *A Visitor's Guide to Historic Abbeville, South Carolina*, by Philip G. Clarke, Jr. Special permission is given by his daughter, Trez Clarke.

ABOUT THE AUTHOR

R. Douglas White grew up in Knoxville, Tennessee. He graduated from Carson-Newman College and took a degree in psychiatric social work from the University of Louisville in 1970. He worked for ten years in mental health centers before going into private practice.

His wife, Laura Kissiah, died suddenly in 1990. Three years later, Doug enrolled at Erskine Seminary and planned to study for one year. After receiving a Master of Divinity degree, he was asked to remain and teach. He served as an associate professor of practical theology and director of spiritual formation. During that time, he was the director of the chapel at Erskine for seven years. Doug established the Julia Rhodes Award for Women in recognition of Service and Leadership.

After twenty years in South Carolina, Doug returned to his hometown of Knoxville, Tennessee. In 2015, he married his beautiful widowed friend, Nancy Dempster Kelly. Their present dog is Daisy, named after the puppy of the infamous Possum of Abbeville, South Carolina.

CPSIA information can be obtained
at www.ICGtesting.com
Printed in the USA
LVHW021026180522
719076LV00010B/441

9 781638 142386